MAKING THE IMPOSSIBLE POSSIBLE

WILLEM NEL

FAITH Story
PUBLISHING
Making God Famous by Telling His story

MAKING THE IMPOSSIBLE POSSIBLE

First edition 2015
ISBN 978-0-620-61442-9

© 2015 Willem Nel

Published by:

Faith Story Publishing
3 Flamink Avenue
Mooivalleipark, Potchefstroom, 2531
PO Box 20288, Noordbrug, 2522

Requests for information should be addressed to:
Faith Story Publishing
PO Box 20288, Noordbrug, 2522

Scripture verses were quoted from the following:
The Message taken from THE MESSAGE © 1993, 1994, 1996, 2000, 2001, 2002; NKJV from NEW KING JAMES VERSION © 1982 by Thomas Nelson, Inc.; The Amplified from THE AMPLIFIED © 1954, 1958, 1962, 1964, 1965, 1987 by the Lockman Foundation; Wuest Translation © Kenneth Samuel Wuest (1893 – 1962); 1956-1959, William B. Eerdman; Phillips Translation © B. Phillips, "The New Testament in Modern English", 1962 edition, published by Harper Collins. Contemporary English Version (CEV) Copyright © 1995 American Bible Society; New Living Translation (NLT): Holy Bible, New Living Translation © 1996, 2004, 2007 by Tyndale House Foundation; The Mirror from THE MIRROR © 2012, used with permission.

I dedicate this book to my parents, Andre and Christine Nel, and parents-in-law, Pieter and Bettie de Vries. The Word they invested into my life helped me believe that God is only good. They are modern day faith heroes.

Disclaimer

This testimony of the transformation of Potchefstroom between 1992 - 2014 is told from my and others' personal experience. It is not meant to be an historical account of everything that happened in Potchefstroom over that time, but it is told from our perspective - this is our story. There were many role-players - people who prayed for the transformation of Potchefstroom and we honor their contributions. Unfortunately, there are still many who do not acknowledge Potchefstroom as a city that models transformation in Africa.

Also, we know that satan is a proper noun that is usually spelled with a capital letter. However, we refuse to honor the enemy in any way which is why satan is written with a small letter.

WHAT OTHERS ARE SAYING

WILLEM NEL LOVES TO ENCOURAGE PASTORS and leaders to believe God for the impossible. Many Sunday mornings — no matter where I am in the world — I receive a text from him that stretches my faith and encourages my heart. That's why I can't think of a better person to write *Making the Impossible Possible*. May this book encourage you to fully trust God all day, every day, and in every situation you might face.

Pastor Steve Murrell
President of Every Nation Ministries, Author
& Accidental Missionary

I HAVE HAD THE PRIVILEGE OF KNOWING Willem Nel personally and professionally for many years. Walking with him through many seasons gave me inside access to who he is and how he lives. His new book, *Making the Impossible Possible*, is more than a good read, it's his life message. He is a man of authentic faith. The words on each page are what he has believed, acted upon, proven and passed on to others. His person, family and ministry are loaded with the evidences of heaven's currency, faith, creating powerful exchanges between a good God and a fallen world. I highly recommend his book to anyone needing greater revelation, activation and application of the God kind of faith.

Dr. Bill Bennot
Senior Pastor Journey of Grace, Author of
Unstoppable Kingdom

THIS IS MY PRIVILEGE to be able to endorse this book for the man of God, Pastor Willem. If there is anyone in this world who could write a book about impossible situations, it is surely Pastor Willem, because he has been there, seen it and survived it.

His story and testimony alone are enough to inspire faith in anyone going through a hard time, so I highly recommend this book for anyone passing through any difficult situation and in any case, difficult times come in the life of everybody, so everybody will benefit from this book.

Pastor Sunday Adelaja
Founder and Senior Pastor of the Embassy of God, Author

THE BOOK INSPIRED AND TURNED INTO REALITY by Pastor Willem Nel is very fittingly called *Making the Impossible Possible*. These words are probably the best encapsulation of the qualities that he brings to his ministry and hence to the book which is grounded so strongly in what he believes in and lives in practice in every facet of his life. He lives and is driven by a faith that is in the most profound sense of the word *active* – a faith that is postulated on doing what needs to be done to build the kingdom of God, to convince people to embrace this faith and to join in love, compassion and humility in the work of God upon earth. His faith has been tempered like steel in the crucible of earthly suffering and setbacks, but he has not deviated from the true course. And his message remains simply to listen to God's Word, to remain active and to build – to build the city that God has guided him to, to engage others in the same vision and to inspire them to build with him to the greater glory of the Lord who is his Guide, his Solace and his Beacon of Light. *Making the Impossible Possible* takes the reader on a journey of amazing miracles, possibilities and insights. I recommend this to anyone interested in growing in God's presence.

Professor Annette Combrink
Former Campus President of the Northwest University (Potchefstroom Campus) as well as former Mayor of Tlokwe Municipality

MAKING THE IMPOSSIBLE POSSIBLE is a book that unpacks what faith is and why faith is necessary. Willem has done an incredible job in teaching the church about faith for many years and this book captures scriptures, stories and testimonies of people impacted by this very essence of our Christian belief, Faith in God. Someone once said "Stories give us tools to understand life". This book gives us tools to understand God, His will and His promises for our lives.

Pastor Simon Lerefolo
His People Joburg, Heartlines Chairperson, Director at AGES (Africa Geo-Environmental & Engineering Science) and Director at Engage Entertainment

I HAVE KNOWN WILLEM FOR OVER A DECADE and have heard him preach and live the message of faith. Willem has many great messages, but this, no doubt, has been the anthem of his life and has greatly impacted me personally. I have watched him bringing the reality of heaven down to the natural circumstances of life – be it with financial challenges, healing or impossible situations. I know that you will be inspired and challenged to grow spiritually as you read through the testimonies and apply the principles recorded in this book.

Pastor Gilian Davids
Lead Elder: His People Churches – Cape Town

WILLEM NEL KNOWS FIRST-HAND if you can see the invisible, you can do the impossible. In this book, *Making the Impossible Possible*, he teaches how to lay hold of the promises of God for whatever impossible situation you face. Read this book and live with new fervour and faith!

Pastors Ron & Lynette Lewis

WILLEM NEL HAS BEEN A VERY DEAR FRIEND of mine for nearly a decade. If I could use one word to describe his life, it's a life walked by "faith". His book, *Making the Impossible Possible*, is not merely a work of intellectual theology, but rather ordinary people who stepped out, believed for the impossible and saw it happen!

From overcoming an almost incurable disease, to believing for funds to fulfill his son's lifelong dream to attend ORU, Willem has personally witnessed the miraculous. By faith, it is possible to please God, and faith is possible to everyone. Willem truly is a man who pleases God and can wondrously testify to his faithfulness! This is his story and the story of many others who have personally witnessed the mighty power of God.

Pastor Bubba Mccann
Lead pastor, Our Savior's Church

OVER THE YEARS, I HAVE KNOWN WILLEM to be a man of faith. His life and ministry are testaments of the authenticity of the life of faith. In *Making the Impossible Possible*, my friend Willem Nel has captured the message of faith in a simplified and easily applicable manner. This book will inspire you to greater things for God and activate in you an appetite for the faith that makes the impossible possible.

Pastor Eric Bapetel
Lead Pastor, Every Nation Midrand, Author of
Supernatural Immunity

WILLEM NEL IS THE ONE MAN I KNOW on planet earth who is a living, breathing miracle. Like diamonds forged under pressure, his insights come from a deep and precious place. Your faith will not be the same after reading the stories, testimonies, and works of God in *Making the Impossible Possible*.

Pastor Kenny Luck
Author of *Sleeping Giant*, President, Every Man Ministries

IN WILLEM NEL'S SECOND BOOK, *Making the Impossible Possible*, we understand the significance of the mustard seed. In an era where postmodernism and skepticism have challenged many people's faith in God, this book brings so much clarity and hope. In a very practical way, Nel weaves the truth of Scripture with stories from his own life as well as stirring testimonies from the lives of others. It is a fresh, applicable outlook on life from someone who does not make faith a cheap add-on but who views faith as the heartbeat of every believer. I personally know Willem Nel as man of deep faith who has an unshakable trust in God. His life is an example of practical faith and selfless sacrifice in building God's Kingdom.

When he exposes the "Faith Thieves" in Chapter 8, you as reader will quickly identify how we are so often suffocated by the lies of the enemy. Willem breaks open the Word so simply and clearly that you won't just gain head knowledge of the Word, but also the ability to apply it practically in order to grow in faith. In faith, I look forward to seeing the fruit this book will yield in the history of our country!

Retief Burger
Singer, Writer and Church Leader

FOR ME, WILLEM NEL AND THE STORY of his life is an evidence of the statement he made in this book: "when you hear God's Word and it starts coming alive in you, it becomes a reality to you." In spite and within circumstances tempting to contradict God's promises, he preached and kept the Word close to him like Jesus did. He gives value to the topic "making the impossible possible" by sharing his stories with us in this book. Being close to him over years, I can witness that he is a man of faith, understanding the gift of grace, motivated to activate faith in others and tested/trained to a level of a practitioner of patience! May the words in this book be a tool to activate Word in the lives of many!

Dr Stephan Pretorius
Senior Geo-Environmental Scientists, Geologist
& Project Manager

WE LIVE IN CHALLENGING TIMES! If pastors and leaders are to successfully navigate and build prevailing churches and ministries in the 21st century, the timeless message of *faith* is an indispensable tool in every leader's toolbox. In the age of post-modernism and pre-Christianity... yes... that's what I said, faith must be at the core of passion and at the forefront of vision. *Making the Impossible*

Possible is a must-read if you want to learn more about the miracle working, transformative nature of faith. Willem Nel is a man of faith! His life and ministry in Potchefstroom, South Africa is living proof that one faith-filled man can make a difference.

Pastor Randy Craighead
Executive Pastor Church of the King, Mandeville, Louisiana

I HAVE KNOWN PS WILLEM NEL for over 10 years and during this time I have come to know him as a man of faith. He not only writes and preaches faith but lives and exemplifies it's reality. In the pages of this book you will learn the principles of a life of faith written by someone who has faced the impossible and experienced the God that makes all things possible. Prepare for a faith injection!

Dr Serge Solomons
MD(Wits), Ordained minister (Every nation), Executive Leadership Coach (TLI)

PASTOR WILLEM NEL CARRIES A WORD OF FAITH like few others. I have had the great honor of walking with him for many years as a close friend, and have seen him live all that he preaches and teaches here. This book powerfully breaks open the Word and imparts a break through faith! Thank you Willem for all you bring to the body of Christ in this key revelation.

Pastor Roger Pearce
Lead Elder His People Joburg, Team leader Every Nation Southern Africa

MAKING THE IMPOSSIBLE POSSIBLE is a fresh reminder to us all that we have been called to "do the impossible." Willem reminds us, of the God that calls things that do not exist into existence. Cantered on the Word of God and laced with dynamic, real life testimonies each chapter inspires the reader to develop their faith and do the seemingly impossible. One thing will be clear as you read ... Willem is a man that oozes the message of faith. He has lived it. It has worked. Read and be blessed.

Pastor Russ Austin
Lead Pastor Southpoint Community Church, Jacksonville, Florida, US

MAKING THE IMPOSSIBLE POSSIBLE IS A BOLD declaration of our New Testament inheritance. Each testimony resonates with God's goodness and grace that He made available to us in Christ Jesus.

In this book, Willem Nel does not give us a theoretical rhetoric about faith, but as someone who has personally wrestled through these principles, he writes from experience to help us understand the process more easily. This book will help you better comprehend the finished work of Christ within the context of every challenge you face in life.

Pastor Alan Platt
Leader: Doxa Deo Ministries

WILLEM NEL'S LIFE IS MARKED WITH an authority to write about faith as a result of his life experience. His supernatural recovery from sickness taught him to "see the unseen" (Heb 11:1). He writes passionately about his faith experiences, as Phillip Yancey describes: "I have learned that faith means trusting in advance what will only make sense in reverse". Things that most people would describe as ordinary or normal, Willem recognizes with conviction that God is up to something great. This book will teach you to expect the best in life and to confidently take risks, seeing things from God's perspective. Willem's passion for faith and his interpretation of God's promises in His Word, will challenge you to embrace a life-changing journey of faith!

Dr. Paul Smit
Relational Specialist, Life Coach, Organizational Health Consultant

THIS INSPIRING BOOK IS ALL ABOUT people placing their faith in the infallible goodness and faithfulness of God and how this opens doors to the miraculous in their lives. Willem Nel shows extraordinary insight in the midst of various challenges and shows us practically how he overcame them, ultimately leading to the transformation of a city. He also gives the reader a Biblical perspective on faith and how it can be lived out practically. This is one of those books that every believer should read in order to challenge our faith and to grow so we can truly experience the reality of God's provision.

Dr. Ernrich F. Basson
Senior Leader Collage Church Pretoria, Extraordinary Senior Lecturer North West University (NWU)

THIS BOOK RIGHTLY HIGHLIGHTS THE FACT that faith is the opposite of fear, which is extremely relevant and necessary in South Africa's current context. You will definitely be encouraged when you read the various testimonies in this book. The faith principles, which are thoroughly yet simply explained, come straight out of the Word of God. Get these principles into your spirit and experience the absolute goodness of God – even in challenging times.

Willem Nel grew up in front of me. He is one of my spiritual sons and it is a privilege for me to write the foreword of this book. I am thankful to see these principles of faith, which have been built into him over many years, form part of such an insightful book about faith. The fact that Willem has successfully applied these principles in his own personal life so many times, adds credibility to this book. It is, therefore, not merely head knowledge, but an authentic life experience of the goodness and faithfulness of God. I know this book will be a great blessing to everyone who reads it.

Pastor Ronnie Barnard
Senior pastor Word and Life Church, Apostolic Leader of Word and Life Network, Author

WILLEM NEL SUCCEEDS IN TAKING THE STORIES of ordinary people who we encounter on a daily basis and making their stories so accessible and easy to relate to that we, as readers, are able to identify and live our own stories through them. By exploring timeless Biblical and Christian themes through a completely fresh perspective, we experience something of God's great love for His creation – and yes, even for those who are often perceived to be on the outskirts of society who dream of being able to taste the grace and favor of God. In reading this book, as is the case with many other faith stories, this principle stands out: "Let's talk about it once you have personally experienced it!" It is particularly refreshing to hear the evangelistic truths expressed honestly and without compromise as though you are hearing them for the first time. It makes us stand in awe of God's love, healing and comfort once again. It is clear that Willem Nel, under the leading of the Holy Spirit, shows a sensitivity to the city God called him to, as well as her people, which makes this book so much more effective in giving people hope. As you begin reading, you will quickly discover that this book calls you deeper into a conversation with God. Or possibly rather "a journey together with God."

Rev. Johan Raubenheimer
NG Church Potchefstroom-North

IT IS A JOY AND A PRIVILEGE to whole-heartedly endorse Willem Nel's new book: *Making The Impossible Possible.* For those who seek God and who have found Him, this book will help you discover new sources of power that will go a long way in helping you cope with the everyday challenges of life. It creates the possibility of functioning in the freedom of God's grace and truth.

These powerful, practical and absolutely essential revelations from Scripture leads the reader to a place where the Word can become flesh in their everyday lives. Willem reminds us of the unlimited power that we have been blessed with in order to convert God's Word into actions.

I pray that the power of the Good News will explode in the hearts and lives of many. That there will be a new revelation that God is a God of faith, grace and miracles. That the spiritual well-being of each person who reads this book will grow with great wisdom.

Prof. Deon de Klerk
Professor Emeritus and Former Dean of the Faculty of Economic and Management Sciences. Potchefstroom Campus of the North West University

THANK YOU

THANK YOU IS THE BASIS FOR A LIFE OF FAITH because 'thank you' reminds you of impossible situations where someone else helped make it possible. I want to begin by saying Thank You to my Lord Jesus who I love so much. I want to thank Him for loving me first, for choosing me before I chose Him; to thank Him for life and that He is a God of relationship; for introducing me to others who He loves.

Thank you to the love of my life, Celesté, who chose to take on the impossible with me in Jesus' name. Thank you to each of my children who are all heroes of faith - Guilliam, Charmoré, Annwaniq and D'ianrew.

Thank you to my parents for teaching me to TRUST GOD FOR EVERYTHING. My mom, Christine, for awakening an unshakable faith in me. My parents-in-law Pieter and Bettie De Vries who always demonstrated the life, power and truth of the Word of God, and who live it.

Thank you to my church, His People Faith City (Potchefstroom, Parys, Klerksdorp and Campus). This is your story of the goodness and greatness of God. My Spiritual Family, Every Nation South Africa, who kept encouraging me in times where I didn't think I could face the next giant or impossibility. Roger Pearce, Gilian Davids and Simon Lerefolo, I cannot imagine trying to live a life of faith without spiritual family. Our greater Every Nation family worldwide who gave us the platform to see the nations as our home. Specifically Pastors Steve Murrell, Rice Broocks, Ron Lewis, Russ Austin and Jim Laffoon who invested the Word of God in our lives over many years.

Thank you to the men and women of God who built the Word of faith in me. My spiritual father, Pastor Ronnie Barnard from Word and Life Ministries. I want to make special mention of Prophet Kobus van Rensburg, Frans du Plessis and Ron Kushmael who all inspired a greater level of faith at various stages in our lives.

I want to thank friends who became like family to me through the years. They ministered to me and carried our ministry through prayer and support. I had significant God moments with them - Pastors Steve Robinson, Jacob Aranza, Todd Schumacher and my brother from another mother, Bubba McCann.

Thank you to our Faith Story Publishing Team. The directors, Louise Buys, who helped with the foundation chapters of this book and Morné Vorster, who as Financial Director invested money into this project. Thanks also to the shareholders who all believe in the dream of making God famous.

A big thank you to Prof. Franci Jordaan who acted as shadow writer for this book. She has the ability to rework my sermons and rough content in a way that hooks the reader. What a privilege to work together on this book. I want to thank Louise-Marie Combrink and Prof. Annette Combrink who translated the book into English. Thank you to my son, Guilliam who edited a large portion of this book and who made it internationally friendly. May we write many books together in the future. Thank you to Fiona Matier who was the editor of the English book and who ensured we would print a quality English book. Fi, as always you managed to make "ordinary" material look good.

A special thank you to each person who shared their testimony with me, and with everyone reading this book. I know it wasn't always easy and yet you did it anyway – I sincerely appreciate it.

Thank you to the Holy Spirit who will guide you as reader to discover that God is absolutely good.

A WORD FROM THE AUTHOR

MAKING THE IMPOSSIBLE POSSIBLE IS FOR every person facing a mountain. Perhaps you're facing an impossibility – a situation that others have said cannot be done or there is no solution for what you're going through. This is when you wish someone would step in and solve the problem for you or simply get rid of the giant you're facing, or better still, give you an easy way out. It is in these times, however, that God flexes His muscles and shows you His might and empowers you with His Word to speak to the mountain – be it sickness, a financial crisis, an injustice that is staring you in the face like a Goliath telling you no-one can overpower him – and tell it to move and be thrown into the sea.

I believe that when you're facing a mountain you need to be thankful that YOU of all people on earth have the opportunity to speak to this impossibility and say, "MOVE! GET OUT OF MY WAY!"

At some point in our lives, each one of us will stand before an impossibility. In that moment we have a choice – will we "risk" it to trust God's Word or will we stay in the same place and simply hope the mountain will disappear?

In this book, you as reader will be confronted with the absolute goodness of God. There is never faith without risk. Faith means stepping out into the unknown – a place of trust that you know nothing about. In 2 Corinthians 5:7 it says:

For we walk by faith, not by sight. (2 Corinthians 5:7, NKJV)

This means we look with spiritual eyes and not physical eyes. We view the world from God's perspective and not a human perspective.

The faith that we speak of in this book is a faith that is birthed and anchored exclusively in the unfailing goodness and faithfulness of God – in His character and limitless ability.

You will read my story of how we, as a family, had to trust God to transform a small town into a city. You will hear Louise and Fiona's testimonies of how they stood before armed robbers and confessed God's Word. You will meet Anita and discover that the impossibilities she faced transformed her into a modern day faith giant. So many life-changing, impossible stories, woven together in the revelation and power of God's unfailing Word will make you want to read this book over and over again. My prayer is that you will stand up, take your rightful position and say to the impossible mountain you're facing, "Move and throw yourself into the sea in the name of Jesus Christ."

In this book you will understand that people in South Africa have been bound in a terrible grip of fear. There are people who have given up on the idea of having children, but we have made the choice to hold onto God's Word and believe it above all else – this is why this book contains testimonies from people like Anton and Tania, as well as the Abdalla family who we prayed for to have children. We can joke about it today, but I'm still "tagged" in countless Facebook posts across the world where couples thank us for the Word of Faith we released over them. Read what God says in Jeremiah 29:7 and 11:

Make yourselves at home there and work for the country's welfare. "Pray for Babylon's well-being. If things go well for Babylon, things will go well for you." ...I know what I'm doing. I have it all planned out—plans to take care of you, not abandon you, plans to give you the future you hope for.

Enjoy the book!
Willem Nel

TABLE OF CONTENTS

"What is impossible with men
is possible with God"
(Luke 18:27).

1
WHAT IS FAITH?

WITHOUT FAITH IT IS IMPOSSIBLE to please God. This faith is not a Facebook status or a sports star who points his finger to heaven or makes a gesture of prayer following a successful effort; and neither does this faith refer to a film star or presenter who ends a speech with the words 'God bless you'. No, if you are serious about life, faith is about how you live. You may be reading this book out of curiosity – perhaps someone recommended it to you. You will learn what faith is and what it isn't.

This is a book about FAITH. You will read stories about people who faced the impossible and with a word from God knew that the impossible could become possible.

In the first chapter, I talk about what faith is. Erika and her husband Bernard are, in my mind, two heroes of faith. This was not always the case – their deeply touching story about their baby boy, Retief, awoke in them an unshakable faith in a God who is only good. Here is Erika's story:

My baby only lived for three days. Somewhere between healing and sorrow, dealing with the most profound loss I have ever experienced, I found myself having to make sense of WHAT exactly had happened. Where am I? Where is God? And where do I go from here? My name is Erika and this is my story.

At 34 weeks of pregnancy, complications arose, and an emergency caesarian was necessary. **I did not want to have an early caesarian section.** *I felt trapped, like a caged animal looking for a way out. When Retief was born, I did not hear that anticipated "first cry" everyone talks about, and the silence of those standing around me drove me up the wall. Why isn't he crying? I wanted someone to say something.... My husband Bernard walked towards where the nurses were busy with our child to take a picture of him, but they immediately sent him away. What's going on? They took our baby away and after I was stitched up, we had to wait for two hours to see the pediatrician.*

When we finally talked to the pediatrician, the news was not good. Our baby had an extensive list of medical complications, the most pressing and urgent one being his heart, which was not receiving oxygen-rich blood. We felt paralyzed - overwhelmed by the reality. It was too much, too soon, and too terrible. I wished that all this was just a bad dream, that I could simply blink my eyes, wake up, and go back to the pleasant reality where I was still pregnant, just like it should be. I felt so powerless.

The doctor wanted to have my baby flown to Pretoria where he could receive better medical care, but they needed to stabilize him first. Bernard and I were almost too afraid to go and see our baby, fearing the worst, but we went anyway. He was beautiful - a handsome, perfect little boy. He looked so calm and peaceful. He had wisps of soft hair, the loveliest little mouth, and a well-shaped head. In my eyes, he was perfect.

My heart was breaking. As a mom, the one thing that I

wanted to do was to be able to care for him, to cherish and protect him, but I couldn't. I was desperate to hold him, to tell him that I was here for him, and how sorry I was about everything, but again, I couldn't.

Then the waiting began. Every time we went to see him, we prayed, "God, let your will be done." Sometimes I would pray, "Take him if You know it's for the best." But once we left his side, our prayer would be, "Please heal him."

They called us. His condition was deteriorating. Did we want to be there if something happened? I couldn't. As much as I wanted to be with him and hold his hand, I was not up to simply standing there as life left him – that same life I felt kicking inside me just one day before.

He died that Sunday morning. They brought him to us and for the first time I could hold my baby – only for a short while. This story was only a part of the journey. The longest part of this journey would take place INSIDE of me.

I have to interrupt Erika's testimony here. My wife, Celesté and I visited them in the hospital during that time. We stood with this family, powerless in ourselves and devoid of the faith needed to trust God for a creative miracle. These visits were a turning point for us - first in Celesté and then in me. We would not passively accept sickness and the work of the enemy as a given. But let's get back to Erika and her story:

This was too heavy, too much for Bernard and me to merely "get over". We began to ask questions – which we should have done long before, but you only really begin to take something seriously when it hits too close to home.

We knew that God had not created our son like that. John 10:10 says that the thief does not come but to steal, and to kill, and to destroy. God gives life, and gives it in abundance. Abundance is not a "broken" baby.

I am only sharing the rest of the insight we gained through this experience with Retief six years later, and although it greatly shook my "religious beliefs", we are now living in victory for the first time – as the Word of God promised it should be.

I came to realize that my words were only lip service: "God is great, God is good, God heals, God protects", and so on. However, these words did not change my THOUGHTS or my actions. James writes that faith must give rise to actions. For example: If I say that I believe that God will protect me and that He will charge his angels to deliver and carry me (Ps.91) and yet I am still fearful for WHATEVER reason – whether violence, the future, or issues that relate to my children – then I am merely paying lip service to GOD! If I say that God is great, but my problem or illness (cancer) overwhelms me, then I'm paying God nothing more than lip service!

One of the greatest lies that I was taught by the church while I was growing up was the misconception that we cannot know the will of God for our lives. However, Scripture teaches me exactly what His will for my life is. How can I stand next to Retief's bed and pray, "Your will be done?" God's will is LIFE! And therefore I have to speak life over my child and not wonder whether he should live or die.

James 1:6-8 says that if I am like a wave of the sea that is tossed around and made to doubt, that I cannot receive anything from God. Please note that this does not mean that He does not WANT to give me anything. But I have a choice. In Deuteronomy 30 God says to His people, "I set before you life and death. Therefore, CHOOSE LIFE".

I never understood (as we often think we do) that I also had a part to play by responding to what Jesus had ALREADY done on the cross. The lie had caused me to accept what "God had decided" and stopped me from fighting back. Jesus said on the cross: "It is finished." He has already done all that is needed, and has provided everything we may require. When He ascended to heaven, He gave us His Spirit, so we can now act like Jesus did. 1 John 4:17 says, "As Jesus is, so are we in THIS world". Hallelujah! This is not arrogance – this is Truth. Is it by my own power? No, by His power in me. Ephesians 3:20 says it is according to the power that works in US.

God has chosen to do His work on earth through people, and this is why Jesus had to come to earth as a man (and as God). We are His representatives, but then, strangely, we react with powerlessness and paralysis to situations (as we did with Retief). But I, with the Spirit of God in me, must understand my authority and respond appropriately. James 4:7 says that WE have to resist the devil and Mark says that WE have to instruct the mountain to move itself to the sea.

Was it God's will for Retief to live only for three days? 2 Peter 3: 9 says that it is God's will that all shall repent and turn to Him. Does this always happen? And in verse 13 we read that we have the expectation of a new earth where the will of God shall reign. God's will does not happen automatically on earth, but God's will is FOR us – He is on our side (Romans 8:31). We tend to forget that God said our battle is not against flesh and blood, but in the Spirit. We don't always realize that there is a battle for our lives in the Spirit, and that we DO have the power to defeat the enemy.

And therefore, because we don't live in our authority, the enemy messes with us and we feel like we have to accept it as "the will of God". You've heard the saying that God picks the most beautiful flowers for his kingdom... It is not God's will to give you a baby only to take it away three days later! **Period!** What I need to do is to renew and transform my mind (Romans 12:2) and get free from the hold of religious thinking.

What a loving God we have! He did not leave us to exist on this earth without spiritual power. Now, for the first time in my walk with God, I began to **SEE** His Word – we pray for the sick, for every kind of pain, for those who are lame, blind and deaf – and they are healed. We respond to the Word and it is true!

Faith is to plant the Word of God in your heart (to meditate on it), to believe that it is true, and to respond to it. This is what makes you see. For example: If thieves come into my house at night intending to harm me, I will NOT hide behind the couch and beg them to take what they want, as long as they leave me alone and do not harm me. NO! I will remember the Scriptures I am meditating on, such as 1 John 4:4 that says greater is He that is in you, than he that is in the world, as well as Deuteronomy 28 that says they will come against me in one way, but flee in many ways – and then THEY will regret their decision to enter my house. Instead, they will hide behind MY furniture, begging for THEIR lives!

Can I really say a thing like this? Yes, God's Word says that when you believe, so shall it be with you.

David only had 5 small stones.
Daniel held the key to the mouths of the lions.
Joshua only needed to shout at the thick walls of Jericho,
which crumbled at his command.
Moses merely had to raise his staff, and the sea opened.
Abraham was 100 years old when his son was born and
the promise of his descendants was thus fulfilled.
   As for me? I will never again allow my baby to
die as if I lacked a stone, a key, a voice, a staff or
a promise...

This is Erika's testimony. She is a phenomenal woman. All of us are confronted with good and bad things in our lives. In this book I want to help you to learn how to trust God, with the help of His Word. This is what we call faith. After the traumatic events surrounding Retief's death, Bernard and Erika could easily have blamed themselves, or they could have lost their faith in God and blamed the world around them for everything that had happened. However, the exact opposite happened – they stood up in faith, and walked the journey of faith with the Lord. The consequences of this decision are visible in their lives, and I can only describe it as remarkable. If we were to think about what had transpired realistically, it would seem that Bernard and Erika faced the impossible –how does one stand up in the midst of such trauma? God made the impossible possible and began to use them actively in His kingdom. This brings me to the following question:

What is Faith?

When we hear the word *faith*, it is often in the context of other words such as church, mosque, cathedral, or religion, but actually this tiny word fits as easily and as well into other spheres of society. The Oxford Dictionary of US English provides these four

definitions for the word *faith*:
1. Complete trust or confidence in someone or something
2. Strong belief in God or in the doctrines of a religion, based on spiritual apprehension rather than proof
3. A system of religious belief: *the Christian faith*
4. A strongly held belief or theory: *the faith that life will expand until it fills the universe*

A brief summary of these definitions would amount to faith simply meaning "to trust" or to "count on". The author of Hebrews describes faith as follows:

> **Now faith is the substance of things hoped for, the evidence of things not seen.** (Hebrews 11:1; NKJV)

Faith thus means to be certain that you can trust someone or something. Faith means trusting in something that I still hope for, but I cannot yet see. The world tends to view faith like this: "If I cannot see or feel it, then I don't believe it happened". However, God says: "If you trust before you see or feel something, you will see your miracle revealed". Let me explain this another way: When someone pays me for something that I sold to him, I don't have to believe (trust) that he will bring me the money, because it has already happened – I can see the money in my hand. On the other hand, we can speak of faith when I sell something to somebody and then I have to trust him if he promises to pay the money the next day – without anything in my hand to see or feel.

Faith is not the consequence of me diligently studying what it means, or even faithfully practicing spiritual principles. Faith is a gift from God – we see this clearly in Ephesians 2:8-9:

> **For by grace you have been saved through faith,**

and that not of yourselves; it is the gift of God, not of works, lest anyone should boast. (Ephesians 2:8-9, NKJV)

We did not receive faith from God because we deserved it, or because we were worthy of possessing faith. No. It is not of us, but of God. We did not obtain faith by our own power or by our own free will. It was simply given to us by God, together with His grace, according to His holy plan and purpose, and as a result, He receives all the glory. Let's pause for a moment and consider the question, "What is Faith?" I want to explain the answer to you by means of two faith statements:

- Faith stretches my imagination
- Faith means taking initiative

Faith STRETCHES my imagination

In Ephesians 3:20 we read the following:

Now to Him who is able to do exceedingly abundantly above all that we ask or think, according to the power that works in us. (Ephesians 3:20, NKJV)

What is the most amazing thing you would want to happen in your life? In this verse, God says to you, "I can surpass anything you can think of! You ain't seen nothing yet! No matter how amazing the thing is you're thinking of – I can and will surpass it!"

Genesis 15 is an example of this first principle that faith begins where your imagination is stretched. Faith always begins with an idea, a concept, a vision, a dream, a spiritual image, or a picture. God said to Abraham one day, "Abraham, I will make you the father of a great nation. You will have many children." Abraham found it very difficult to believe these words at that point in his life. He was already in his nineties, ready to start making plans for his hundredth birthday. Abraham had no children and yet God told him that he would be the father of a great nation. I'm quite sure that Abraham must have thought, "Lord, I really don't know if this prediction is accurate, but if You say so, I'll believe You!" The Lord must have seen the doubt written all over Abraham's face, and therefore He decided to show Abraham a picture. We read the following in Genesis 15, from verse 1:

God begins by stretching our imagination – by giving us a dream, or a vision.

After these things the word of the Lord came to Abram in a vision, saying, "Do not be afraid, Abram. I am your shield, your exceedingly great reward." But Abram said, "Lord God, what will You give me, seeing I go childless, and the heir of my house is Eliezer of Damascus?" Then Abram said, "Look, You have given me no offspring; indeed one born in my house is my heir!" And behold, the word of the Lord came to him, saying, "This one shall not be your heir, but one who will come from your own body shall be your heir." Then He brought him outside and said, "Look now toward heaven, and count the stars if you are able to number them." And He said to him, "So shall your descendants be." And he believed in the Lord, and He accounted it to him for righteousness.
(Genesis 15:1-6, NKJV)

Here the Lord says to Abraham, "I want you to use your imagination

– actually, stretch your imagination. Look at the stars. See if you can count them – that's how many descendants you will have." As I have said, faith always begins with an idea, a concept, a vision, a dream, a spiritual image or a picture. For this reason, the Lord gave Abraham something that he could visualize. Every evening when he wondered around outside, he looked at the heavens and said, "All of these will be my family!" And this is exactly what happened, because the whole of Israel are descendants of Abraham.

God begins by stretching our imagination – by giving us a dream, or a vision. What you can believe, you can achieve. Faith is therefore about visualizing the future in the now. This is exactly what we did with the garbage dumps in our town, Potchefstroom. We saw a future where children would not play or scavenge in these hazardous places. This is my testimony about our vision:

The dream of doing something amazing for God had been brewing in me for a long time. When I was still in the 11th grade, I believed that one day I would be president of my country. However, God had different plans for me. He wanted to turn my heart towards what He held most dear.

In the King James Version and The Message Translation we read the following in Matthew 6:33:

But seek ye first the kingdom of God, and his righteousness; and all these things shall be added unto you.

Steep your life in God-reality, God-initiative, God-provisions. Don't worry about missing out. You'll find all your everyday human concerns will be met.

God loves towns and cities. *He wants us to present these places to Him as living sacrifices. When the Lord called my wife, Celesté and I to Potchefstroom, we were quite reluctant – I particularly did not like the idea at all. I had a music business in Johannesburg, and always felt that I was called to work in the city – the countryside was simply too slow for my taste. However, Celesté had always known that the Lord had called her for ministry. The Lord gave us a very clear Word that He has called us to build bridges between people of all races, generations, and between congregations. We also understood clearly that we were to minister a Word of righteousness to a staunchly conservative faith community. God is merciful and He used many people and conferences to teach us His word and to prepare us for this task. These are some of the problems we experienced in the town that God placed us in:*

- *Great poverty, especially among the black community.*
- *Extreme racism, especially from the students who attended the Agricultural College – they would drive around town at night, looking for black people to harass, then beat them with horsewhips (among other things) – and the police did nothing to stop them.*
- *The town was split by politics and religion.*
- *Economic development was stilted. The primary motivation of the town's founders was that they wanted to guard the feeling of quality, and the peace and quiet of the town. This attitude meant, however, that a small minority grew rich and the rest of the community suffered. At one stage, the lecturers of the local university (a significant number of people in the*

town work for the university) were paid among the lowest wages in comparison to other South African universities.

One of the most significant events we experienced was when Annette Venter, a social worker at the time, took me and a few other ministers to the town's garbage dumps to show us the appalling conditions there.

I was quite overwhelmed. People lived there and ate from the garbage. I just knew we had to do something about it.

We began with a relief program where we would hand out food to the people living there once a week, and later we extended the program to hand out food more regularly. We found out that the community living on the dumps actually came from a place called Sonderwater (literally meaning "without water"). To make matters worse, this community lived on top of a hazardous dolomite area. Because these living conditions made the people so sick, they brought disease to the rest of the community and also to the towns near this area.

We then realized that we could not continue to provide food at the dumps and moved our feeding program elsewhere, but the roads were becoming practically inaccessible. The new place where the children and elderly people received food was close to a water tower.

The Lord spoke to us from Isaiah 58:9-12. I quote from The Message:

If you get rid of unfair practices, quit blaming victims, quit gossiping about other people's sins, If you are generous with the hungry and start giving yourselves to the down-and-out,

Your lives will begin to glow in the darkness; your shadowed lives will be bathed in sunlight.

I will always show you where to go.

I'll give you a full life in the emptiest of places - firm muscles, strong bones.

You'll be like a well-watered garden, a gurgling spring that never runs dry.

You'll use the old rubble of past lives to build anew, rebuild the foundations from out of your past.

You'll be known as those who can fix anything, restore old ruins, rebuild and renovate, make the community livable again.

You'll be known as those who can fix anything, restore old ruins, rebuild and renovate, make the community livable again.

This Scripture has become a motto for us! We experienced a myriad of miracles. We often saw how our food simply multiplied. We helped build schools and churches in the area, and also established a number of vegetable gardens to create a sustainable food source.

At the time I also became involved with a Mayoral committee that was made up of spiritual leaders from all the communities of Potchefstroom. We often had meetings with the executive mayor, Mr. Satish Roopa. He professed to be an Agnostic Hindu, but this did not stop me from regularly praying for him. I invited him and his family to our church and specially extended an invitation to a conference we were hosting called "Hope Again". The *theme of this conference was to "Hope Again" and the subtitle was, "God has not pulled the plug on South Africa – Where there is a climate of Hope, people will believe again."*

This conference took place at a time when the world, and many Christians, had actually given up on hope for South Africa. To grow a congregation in a primarily student-driven community, where one is constantly faced with the impossible, made us more determined to rebuild and restore our community to reflect God's original purpose for this place.

I spoke to Mr. Roopa during one of these committee meetings and we talked about the problems we saw at the garbage dumps. He agreed with me, but he also said that his hands were tied because of issues surrounding the administration of that piece of land. Apparently, that land was not under the town council's administration as it was part of another constituency. And so they were unable to move the dumps. I still remember this as if it happened *yesterday. I said to Mr. Roopa, "Let's pray together about this." He allowed me to do so, slightly reluctantly. My prayer was somewhere along the lines of "Lord Jesus, in Your name I ask that You will move the garbage dumps. Help the mayor and give him sound plans." You see, I believed that faith like a mustard seed could move mountains.*

Two years later, I attended a conference presented by the town council and Mr. Roopa. The conference followed the declaration of Potchefstroom as a green city (i.e. an environmentally-friendly city). I received these photographs from Mr. Roopa:

Left to right: Satish Roopa, Willem Nel, Bill Bennot and Japie Fransman

Like the mountains that Jesus talked of, the garbage dumps PHYSICALLY moved – 3 miles further to a site where access was controlled. Our town also now had a properly registered dumpsite. The site where the people from

Sonderwater lived, and where so many children played in disastrously unsafe conditions, had been cleaned and repurposed. This generated hope in many people and the story touched people around the world. Leaders listened to the testimony and determined to transform their cities in the same way. Further on in this book I will share about the effect of the impossible, and how to grow a city.

Faith, therefore, stretched our imagination and made it possible for us to see the future in the now!

Faith means taking INITIATIVE

In the book of Mark, chapter 5, we read the story of the hemophiliac woman who had been suffering from this condition for twelve years.

> ***Now a certain woman had a flow of blood for twelve years, and had suffered many things from many physicians. She had spent all that she had and was no better, but rather grew worse.*** (Mark 5:25-26, NKJV)

She was never able to stop the bleeding. Of course, this made her unclean in the context of Jewish culture. Consequently, she was not allowed to appear in public among other people – and hence she had no social life. But one day, she heard that Jesus Christ was coming to her town. She said to herself, "If only I can touch his clothes, I will be healed." She took the courageous and daring step of appearing in public – in other words, she took the initiative. Forcing her way through a crowd of people, she finally found herself standing behind Jesus, where again, she took the initiative to touch his garment – and immediately she was healed.

The garbage dumps before transformation

The same site after transformation

Jesus also felt her touch of faith and therefore He asked, "Who touched My clothes?" But there was a multitude of people, all pushing and moving towards Him. The woman herself had to force her way through the crowd – practically crawling through everyone to get to Him. Peter, the rather outspoken disciple, said to Jesus, "You see the multitude surrounding you, and yet you ask, 'Who touched Me?'" But Jesus knew that her touch was different. Initially the woman trembled in fear when she realized that Jesus indeed felt the difference, and therefore she fell onto her knees in front of Him, and told Him her story. And Jesus said to her, "Daughter, your faith has made you whole. Go in peace, and be healed from your disease!"

She took the initiative. She broke the rules. She transgressed the boundaries set by her culture. She pushed through the crowd and took the initiative upon herself – this was the act of faith by which she was healed. Faith, therefore, is the decision to begin, to set things into motion. It means committing yourself to action. Faith is therefore the antidote to procrastination.

If I can return, for a moment, to my testimony about the garbage dumps, I can say this: I also had to take the initiative to start addressing the issue, even under circumstances that simply did not seem to promise any solution.

2

GOD'S GIFT OF GRACE

IN CHAPTER 1, WE READ ERIKA'S extraordinary testimony. There is no doubt that God is good – He is only good. My aim is for God's goodness to overwhelm you. It is His goodness that causes people to repent and turn their lives around. His goodness causes you to think differently and brings you greater insight. His goodness declares that He loves you so much, and this love drives out punishment and fear.

In this chapter you will encounter Anita's story. Her story is so extraordinary you may well think she should never have made it – and yet she did. Her life was changed by God's gift of grace. When you are faced with the impossible, it does not help to recall all the things that you have done wrong. This is when you need to experience something really good - you need to experience God's gift of grace.

The story of Jonah is a very well-known story in the Bible. It is an amazing account of God's compassion, goodness and love for mankind. God felt such compassion towards the people of Nineveh that He did everything in His power to send his messenger, Jonah, to the city. Initially, it is not clear why Jonah had to spend exactly three days inside the fish. I sometimes wonder if Jonah had been quicker in confessing his sins whether God would have sent the fish towards dry land sooner? I know that I would be begging God to let me out of there the minute the fish swallowed me! Can you imagine the horrid smell? Suddenly you find yourself in overwhelming darkness and part of a fish's digestive system! I am sure God could have sent that fish towards dry land sooner, but when Jonah emerged as a life-saver for the people of Nineveh after three days inside the fish, he immediately pointed to Christ. After three days in the grave, Christ brought salvation to all people.

> *For as Jonah became a sign to the Ninevites, so also the Son of Man will be to this generation.* (Luke 11:30, NKJV)

The people of Nineveh confessed their sin, and God in His love and goodness, could not contradict His own nature and immediately extended His grace and compassion to each and every person and saved the city from destruction.

When Christ died for us on the cross, and rose from the grave three days later, the goodness of God became a tangible reality – not only for the people we read about in the Bible, but for you and me. The compassion God feels for us is overwhelming. As a result of the Fall, we not only find ourselves in the same position as the people of Nineveh, but we have also missed out on the original position, plan and relationship that God had in mind for us.

> *So God created man in His own image; in the image of God He created him; male and female He created them. Then God blessed them, and God said to them, "Be fruitful and multiply; fill the earth and subdue it; have dominion over the fish of the sea, over the birds of the air, and over every*

living thing that moves on the earth." (Genesis 1:27-28; NKJV)

God made each of us in His image, unlike any other part of creation. Every time God looks at us, He sees a reflection of Himself as in a mirror. We are now a new creation, we are of the God-kind. The Word teaches us that God created mankind in order to reflect His image on earth. He created us with the ability to reign and we have been appointed as kings to rule over all of creation. We were created as the crown, as the very best part of His creation. Adam and Eve walked with God in the cool of the day without any shame. They

> **We are now a new creation, we are of the God-kind**

experienced the fullness of what God intended for each of us - the totality of a complete and intimate relationship with God and with each other. They experienced a level of intimacy that I desire for myself and for you reading these words. This is certainly possible and it is what God desires for each of us. Adam and Eve enjoyed perfect health, provision and kingship on the earth and they also knew exactly what it meant to live in unbroken fellowship with their Creator and Father. They understood the perfection of God's Kingdom and His reign on earth.

One day, satan spoke to Eve through a serpent. Satan had a cunning plan to deceive Adam and Eve. The plan was executed by causing Eve to doubt her identity, and in this way causing her to doubt whether she could really believe in God.

Then the serpent said to the woman, "You will not surely die. For God knows that in the day you eat of it your eyes will be opened, and you will be like God, knowing good and evil." (Genesis 3:4-5; NKJV)

"Eve, are you sure God is not keeping something really good from you? Are you quite sure that God only has the very best in mind for you? How certain are you that you can trust God, or is it possible that He is making you blind to certain things? Don't you know that you can be like God?" I can imagine how these whispered accusations sowed suspicion in Eve's mind. Such a liar! Eve had already been created in God's image. Her identity as God's image-bearer and as royal ruler on earth had already been undeniably established. And yet the enemy was able to cause her to doubt these things. To make matters worse, God had already established His plan for mankind – a plan of unconditional goodness – for man to be fruitful, to multiply and to reign on earth. Again, the enemy caused Eve to doubt God's Word, and caused her to feel uncertain if she could really believe God. Let's have a look at how these lies and devastating consequences of believing them affects this broken world around us. The enemy, who is called the father of lies, uses suspicion, uncertainty and doubt to sow destruction in our lives, as well as the lives of so many around us. Anita was born into this broken world and this is her story:

Rejection weaved its way through my life, even from before I was born. I was born out of wedlock, and I was given up for adoption when I was one year old. People old enough to be my grandparents adopted me. I was frequently bombarded by my mother's complaints that she never wanted to adopt a girl, but she played along with the adoption as a favor to my father. I was lonely growing up, and between the ages of 6 to 11 years old, well-known older boys often sexually molested me. I was always ashamed because of my "old" parents. When I was a teenager, one of my parents died and I was left behind with the other parent who by then had been long addicted to alcohol. Poor domestic circumstances made me flee this house and caused me to become a rebellious teenager. When I became pregnant in my final year of high school, it seemed like this was the "best" thing that could have happened to me. With a history of rejection, a lack of any experience of intimacy or a relationship with God, my life and later my marriage fell apart. Two broken marriage partners damage each other in the worst possible ways, because no person on earth can make you whole.

When I was at the lowest possible point in my life, God intervened and my life began to change radically. Divorce and depression had been added to my list of horrors, but through fire and deep waters God never let go of my hand. I kept growing, stayed close to Him, made better choices and IN Him I was slowly able to trade the face of a victim for that of a child of victory.

There were so many horrific things that surrounded Anita's life – all of which pointed to the possibility that she would remain a victim of the enemy's plans. I am so grateful that she encountered the overwhelming power of God's love and that His goodness set her free. She writes further:

What do I want to say with this? Am I bragging about how I overcame difficult times in order to make your problems seem small? Absolutely not! I want to encourage you by saying that the moment I chose God, He caused all things to work together for the good and He made everything new (Romans 8:28). As a result, the struggle and temptation from the enemy cannot destroy you any longer but rather makes you stronger and prepares you for far greater things. The very thing that was intended to shut your mouth and keep you silent becomes your pulpit where you can broadcast God's goodness to the world!

What a powerful testimony! Anita will pick up her story later in this chapter but for now I want to return to Eve and the serpent. If the enemy succeeds in making us doubt who God created us to be and gets us to doubt whether God can be trusted, then a separation from God or a breach in our relationship will be inevitable. This would result in us missing our purpose and effectiveness on this earth. Our faith or lack of faith in God determines which side of the Fall we will live our lives – whether we live in the perfection of His Kingdom, or whether we are permanently trapped in the flesh and its shortcomings.

Nothing at all promising awaited Adam and Eve on the other side of the fruit – only the shame, guilt and fear that went hand in hand with the Fall shrouded Adam and Eve like a dark cloud. Adam relinquished his right to reign on earth, to satan. As God promised, mankind perished spiritually – eternal death as well as eternity without God threatened all of us. Satan was never really interested in the fruit or whether or not Eve ate the fruit. He was only interested in masterminding the Fall! He knew that the Fall would not just affect Adam and Eve; but all of us, every single person born after them. Yes, that includes you and me. He was purposefully looking to crush the intimacy, powerful partnership and relationship of trust between God and mankind.

Despite this moment of doom and finality in history, this was not the end. God had a plan in place even before the foundations of the earth were created. There could only be one way that the power of sin could be broken - the blood of a sinless, innocent person would have to flow. God then decided to send His Son, Jesus Christ, to the earth in the body of a man. In this way, Jesus, who was the only person without sin, could die in the place of mankind and defeat eternal death, becoming the bridge that would reconcile us – God's children, with Himself. It is almost as if God was so excited about His plan of salvation that He could not stop Himself from referring to it throughout the Old Testament, giving us clues and hints, just like a treasure map would guide you to a hidden treasure.

Adam and Eve tried to hide their nakedness and shame by sewing fig leaves together and covering themselves. God, on the other hand, killed an animal and used the skin to make clothes to cover them. God made provision to cover them by means of a sacrifice. The innocent blood of the animal was a clue, a pointer towards Christ whose innocent blood would flow to redeem every person who had once been guilty of sin.

... and without shedding of blood there is no remission. (Hebrews 9:22b; NKJV)

Many years later, Abraham and Sarah were blessed with a son. Isaac was the son that God had been promising them for so many years, and finally he was born. Can you imagine their joy? Abraham and Sarah were both far too old to bear children and it would have required a miracle for them to conceive a son. We have far greater insight than Abraham and Sarah had with our understanding of modern medicine these days and can truly appreciate the scale of the miracle that actually took place. I can imagine how each time Abraham looked at his son he was reminded of God's faithfulness. Over the years, I have been deeply touched by this story of Abraham. As the leader of a church, I have seen many good friends and members of staff who were unable to have children. I don't believe Abraham's story was included in the Bible for nothing. He is called the father of faith, after all. Anton and Tania were part of our team in Potchefstroom and they trusted God for a child. I simply have to share their story with you:

*On the first day of the ninth month, where 9 symbolizes "fullness" and "completion", God fulfilled His promise when we heard that I was pregnant! But first, we would like to take you with us on our journey of faith that we had to walk before this wonderful news came to us. God gave us a promise seven years ago - a **Word** that contained the names of our children. However, the longer we had to wait, the more difficult it became to keep the fire of our faith burning. In fact, the longer the wait, the greater our testimony would be. And this testimony is, actually, God's story.*

*Since we really had a tough time trying to fall pregnant, we explored a range of expensive medical avenues, treatments and procedures while battling this giant of infertility. God spoke to me again after our last unsuccessful in vitro treatment, telling me to repeat the procedure in **8 months'** time (when we would be in the month of August). At that stage, we did not know about Anton's training period in the USA that lay ahead. And at that stage we were not ready to repeat the trauma of going through the treatment process again. I learnt from Beth Moore's books, however, that **God does not give you tomorrow's grace, or next month's grace today,** and neither does He bestow the grace of another person upon you. When the time is right, His grace will be enough.*

Initially, we set out to "carefully believe", especially in light of our previous disappointments, but we had come to realize that the flames of faith had to be stoked in us. We learnt that it was not enough to simply think about the words we needed to confess, but rather that something supernatural was bound to happen if you expressed your **confession** out loud. This became a daily habit over the next six months. In faith we confessed and we spoke against infertility; we spoke of changing infertility into pregnancy. God also talked to us about our **eating habits and our diets**, especially since I had endometriosis. After we made a few lifestyle changes, we were able to hear the voice of God more clearly.

We even tried to negotiate a little with the Lord, as we believed that things would be simpler if He would help me fall pregnant naturally, but God had another plan. In the words of Pastor Bill Bennot: If your mountain does not move, you may have to climb it. Initially, Anton felt uncertain, but the moment he found peace, I started feeling unsure. We prayed a simple prayer we learnt from Pastor Ronnie Barnard, "Lord, help us in our unbelief." In the middle of our sixth month in the USA we decided to write down our vision. I realized that the month of August was just around the corner, and I felt anxious. I remembered all the negative reports we had received and these thoughts scared me, but thankfully God changed my thought patterns.

I was listening to a sermon by Pastor Russ Austin in the USA, where he spoke of the definition of 'insanity'. He said insanity was doing the same thing over and over and expecting different results. However, he also challenged this statement by saying that a **person CAN do the same thing over and over again and expect different results**, as long as you cast your nets out on God's orders. The Holy Spirit took my breath away, and I personally experienced Him telling me that the next in *vitro treatment would yield different results. Even if I went to the same doctor, even if I got the same hormone shots and even if I waited for the same 10 agonizing days to hear if the procedure had been successful, things would turn out differently this time.*

There was **no special formula** *or glory that marked the doctor or the procedure; the Lord is the One and only Creator of Life, and this time, He performed a miracle inside of me. The two of us now believe in this principle:* ***Simply be obedient to God.***

During this time, we also came to understand the importance of keeping a diary of your walk with God. As we were waiting for the results, fear would often overwhelm me when I wrongfully looked at what I could see with my physical eyes, but Anton would encourage me all the time. I would return to the Word of God and listen to sermons that stirred up my faith (such as the sermon by Pastor Willem that taught us to have David's spirit of victory, not Saul's spirit of fear). This time, the pressure was on God and not on us, which was a huge relief. At our first doctor's visit we told the Lord: "Lord, this is not an easy path, but we just want to obey You – we're doing this for You." What may have felt like a sacrifice released a great ***blessing!***

One of our **steps of faith** *was learning to expect the goodness of God. As we waited for the results of the blood tests, we prepared the nursery – we made up a bed for the baby and hung new curtains. In line with Pastor Willem's sermon series on miracles, we not only spent our time waiting, but we waited in expectation for good to come to us. God also restored our peace. 1 Samuel 1: 15 says: "Hannah poured out her soul to the Lord". The Word* *goes on to say that she walked away with a face that was no longer filled with sorrow (she had been devastated for years as she was unable to have children). Hannah walked away from God's temple filled with **PEACE** – not because her circumstances had changed, but because she had poured out her soul before God. We also learnt to **sow seed** in this time and to **serve** in the midst of the pain we experienced.*

*In **our flesh** we would never have chosen to walk this journey, but looking back at our story with spiritual eyes, we would choose it again. The Lord taught us precious life lessons, all the while carrying us through the difficult times. Our **test** became our **testimony** – one that we share with others, with our little girl Abigail by our side!*

Powerful! Anton and Tania waited and prayed for seven years, and by His goodness God revealed His plan to them. This convinced them that God really is in a good mood – He is not angry with them, and He is not punishing them. He wanted to bless them, as He wanted to bless Abraham. As Anton said, the test became a testimony.

One day, this same God asked Abraham to offer his son Isaac as a sacrifice. This was a test! I probably would have rebuked this thought as being an attack from the enemy - but Abraham got up early the next morning, and took his son, as well as the firewood with him and started to walk. At the halfway mark, Abraham told the servants to stay behind and ensured them that both he and his son would return. At one point, Isaac asked the logical question: "I see fire and wood, but where is the lamb for the burnt offering?" Abraham's answer was simply, "The Lord Himself will provide a sacrificial lamb." When he bound Isaac onto the wood of the altar and prepared to kill him, the Lord spoke to him and said, "Now I know that you fear Me, because you did not withhold your only son from Me." Abraham looked up and saw a ram caught in the thicket by its horns. This ram became the innocent substitute for Isaac. Abraham called the place The-Lord-Will-Provide. Here we see another example of a clue or a pointer to God's sovereign plan of salvation. Just as God provided an innocent ram for the burnt offering, He provided a Substitute for us: Jesus Christ.

When we read about Israel, God's people bound in slavery in Egypt, we see how God flexes His muscles before Pharaoh. He shows who is really in charge, and in one final and powerful deed, Pharaoh's rebellion and stubbornness were dealt with. The night before Israel fled Egypt, God gives us another clue that we read about in Exodus 12. It was time for Israel to pack up and leave Egypt for the land God had promised to Abraham. Israel suffered under the worst kind of slavery and in spite of nine grueling plagues, Pharaoh's heart remained hardened and he would not allow the Israelites to leave under any circumstances. God then gave Moses very specific instructions for the Passover. Every family had to select a year-old, male lamb (or goat) from their herds. This lamb had to be without any defect or blemish, and they had to take good care of it for a few days. They then had to slaughter it and smear the blood on the doorposts of their houses.

It is possible that the head of the house was responsible for making sure the lamb remained spotless and was well cared for during this time. I can imagine how the entire family, especially the small children, would have become quite attached to the lamb.

Four days after each family had selected a lamb, all the households of Israel slaughtered these lambs and smeared their blood onto their doorposts, exactly as God ordered them to do. That night, the angel of death passed through all of Egypt. Where there was no blood applied to the doorposts, the oldest child in each family died. Scripture tells us that there was a child who died in every Egyptian household, but amongst the Israelites, not even a dog barked. The blood was the sign for the angel of death to literally "pass over" that house.

Through the ages, ever since Adam and Eve were bound in the scourge of sin, God has never stopped encouraging man with the hope of His redemption plan.

Jesus was God's choice as the spotless Lamb for His family. Jesus spent two days being interrogated by the high priest Caiaphas, the scribes, the elders and finally by Pontius Pilate, the governor. Nobody could find any fault with Him. He was a blameless Lamb, and therefore, the perfect Sacrifice.

Jesus was crucified. What may seem to have been just another execution, in one moment became the most charged event in all of history. It caused a ripple effect in the spiritual realm that will echo for eternity. The blood that flowed from each painful wound that day has brought salvation to each and every person. The blood of the Lamb saved mankind from eternal death; it washed our sins away and gave us a brand-new position of righteousness.

Let's hear the rest of Anita's testimony. She refers to this testimony as My Story in God's story and it comes from her book *'Die Groter Prentjie'* (meaning *The Bigger Picture*).

We often look at people when they talk about things, and we think: "Easy for you to say. You haven't been in my shoes". If you choose to be a victor instead of a victim, however, you will find yourself in the spiritual gym admiring your muscles. Not because you are so amazing, but because you have chosen God. If you have chosen to be an overcomer, your only battle is exercising your faith muscles to become stronger.

May the love of God, that has made the world go round

since the first days of creation, truly inspire you. May you also allow Him to turn your world around.

*Am I holy? I am, **because God says** in His Word that through Jesus, I am holy! Am I perfect? Yes, **because God says** Jesus came to perfect me! Do I still make mistakes? Absolutely! Although we are no longer of this world, we are still IN this broken world. One thing I know: I press on, I live in MY **righteousness IN Christ**, I leave the things that are behind me and I reach out towards the things that lie ahead. My eyes are fixed on Him, the perfecter of my faith!*

*The moment I realized that this life is not about ME, but about GOD, the whole course of my life changed direction. I understood that I was given the opportunity of being part of God's story, to play my part on His stage and to work with the main character, Jesus Christ, to display His Father's plan for mankind. **His story must be told** in our conversations, in the books we write, the songs we sing and in our theatre productions on stage! **He is the Lamb of God, the King of kings and He is worthy to be praised for evermore!***

It is once again clear from Anita's testimony that God is good. He is always good. He takes our broken lives, saves us from eternal death and makes us righteous. We are righteous through His Son, and this righteousness gives us a platform where we can praise and glorify God's Name!

Some time ago, I heard the story of a high school girl who was a very strong athlete. Her dream was to win the 200m at the South African junior athletics championship (SA's). She worked really hard to fulfill her dream, but in order to qualify for the championships, she first had to run the race in a specific qualifying time at one of the official athletics events. She missed it by a split second. A split second stood between her and her dream of running in her provincial colors.

A season or two later, she completed the 200m in 22 seconds, qualifying her for the SA's. Suddenly, everything changed! Her name appeared on the list of participants, she was awarded provincial colors and she could attach her official computer generated athletes number onto her clothing. She had a place on the bus, and the sixth lane was reserved for her. In other words, her qualifying time gave her a right or a platform, where she could participate in the actual race.

God declared us righteous in Christ, which gives us the right to stand before God once again.

When Jesus blew out his final breath, the temple curtain was torn, symbolically representing the fact that the separation or distance between God and man that had existed since the Garden of Eden was immediately and completely destroyed. God declared us righteous in Christ, which gives us the right to stand before God once again. In other words, in Christ we are qualified to stand before God once again and because Christ took the punishment of our sin upon Himself, we have now been disqualified for all punishment. We can once again enjoy an intimate, dynamic relationship and partnership with Him, walking with Him in the evening breeze, so to speak, as we once did in the Garden. Nothing can separate us from God any longer. No sin or judgment can keep us from His love or remove our position of righteousness.

... giving thanks to the Father, who has qualified you to share in the inheritance of the saints in

the kingdom of light. For he has rescued us from the dominion of darkness and brought us into the kingdom of the Son he loves, in whom we have redemption, the forgiveness of sins (Colossians 1:12-14, NKJV)

Let me introduce the faith process to you. This process will appear in many chapters of the book and will hopefully be something you can easily recognize and remember when you hear the words 'faith process'.

You allow His Word to come close to you

His Word is a light or a revelation to you

The light brings clarity or understanding (your mind understands the revelation)

When you understand you begin to trust

Trust gives you a place to stand

A place to stand gives you a platform

You must decide – will you act or remain passive? Your obedience to the Word that brings light will proceed into action [a deed]. This is a calculated risk that you take, because your trust is in a good and faithful God. Passivity will make you procrastinate and eventually it will make you give up.

"It is finished!" These were His last words before He breathed His final breath. He had done everything that was necessary.

Everything was complete. God kept His promise – the promise He confirmed in various ways throughout the Old Testament. He kept His Word. The circle was complete – from the first two people who stumbled into sin, to all of humanity born into sin, who have the opportunity to be reconciled with their heavenly Father in a single moment.

Even the law was fulfilled! For years and years after Adam and Eve attempted to cover their own shame by stitching fig leaves together, people have been trying to cover up their own sins, depending on their own ability to do so. People have also tried to make themselves acceptable to God by keeping to the letter of the law. Isn't this what we sometimes do, even today? Try and be acceptable to God based on our good deeds?

"It is finished!" These were His last words before He breathed His final breath. He had done everything that was necessary.

The exclusive purpose of the law was to show people that it would be impossible to reach God's standards, and it was never meant to be a way towards God.

What shall we say, then? Is the law sin? Certainly not! Indeed I would not have known what sin was except through the law. For I would not have known what coveting really was if the law had not said, "Do not covet." ... Once I was alive apart from law; but when the commandment came, sin sprang to life and I died. (Romans 7:7,9; NKJV)

And for those who felt that they weren't doing too badly in their attempts to live by the law, Jesus raised the bar even higher:

> *"You have heard that it was said to the people long ago, 'Do not murder, and anyone who murders will be subject to judgment.' But I tell you that anyone who is angry with his brother will be subject to judgment. Again, anyone who says to his brother, 'Raca, ' is answerable to the Sanhedrin. But anyone who says, 'You fool!' will be in danger of the fire of hell."* (Matthew 5:21-22; NKJV)

Jesus made it abundantly clear that there was no way on earth that anyone of us could become acceptable before God by doing the right things and earn our salvation. In this same conversation, Jesus told the people that He did not come to do away with the law, but to fulfill it. Jesus came on behalf of us to meet God's standards and to fulfill the law.

After three days in the grave, Jesus was victorious over the greatest enemy of all: death. He rose from the dead, ascended to heaven, and now sits at the Father's right hand.

In this position of power and authority, He won the victory for us as the Head of the body, or the Church, not only so we would be reconciled with God forever, but also so we could reign as kings on earth.

> *But because of his great love for us, God, who is rich in mercy, made us alive with Christ even when we were dead in transgressions —it is by grace you have been saved. And God raised us up with Christ and seated us with him in the heavenly realms in Christ Jesus, in order that in the coming ages he*

might show the incomparable riches of his grace,
expressed in his kindness to us in Christ Jesus.
(Ephesians 2:4-7, NKJV)

In His Son, Jesus Christ, God has also restored His original calling for us on earth. As the body of Christ, we are seated with Him in heavenly places and we rule and reign with Him. We are, therefore, no longer subject to the authority of sin but are free and empowered to work with Jesus in order to actively advance God's kingdom on earth without doubt or fear of any kind.

Through His death and resurrection, Jesus wrote us into His inheritance in the form of the New Testament. The only requirement for a person's will to come into effect is when the person who has undersigned that will or testament has died. God's will, the totality of His property and promises, was bestowed on us as His beneficiaries the moment when Jesus called out "It is finished!" Every prayer contained in this will applies to us and there is nothing we can do to earn it. The content of a will goes to the beneficiary – undeservingly so!

What God gave us through Jesus Christ was an act of pure grace. By grace, God unfolded His Redemptive Plan and all that it contained. God's grace is His undeserved favor that He generously bestows upon us. God's grace is a gift to us that we could never earn.

Let's consider the idea of a gift for a moment. I'm crazy about technology. One of the technological wonders that I really admire is the Apple iPad. As a father of a family of six, I am used to working hard, saving and managing a budget in order to take care of my family in the best possible way. When it came to the iPad, things were no different – I could not afford it at the time. However, I kept an eye on prices, compared different outlets, and put some money away in order to see if there was any chance I would be able to buy it for myself.

One day as I was talking to a friend, he told me that he had been thinking of giving me a gift for quite some time. He didn't know anything about the desire in my heart and yet he asked me, "How would you feel about an iPad?" You can imagine how I felt! I was ecstatic, and in that moment I remembered how wonderful it is to receive a gift, especially if it's something you want really badly. You don't have to work or budget for a gift, and you don't have to earn it.

A gift is just what it says – simply something that is given to you. It is something that someone else selected for you and paid for in full before they gave it to you. You don't have to pay anything for it. All you have to do is receive it.

When we stand before God, we usually want to take the responsibility on ourselves to work hard and score points so we can earn God's blessings.

For it is by grace you have been saved, through faith –and this not from yourselves, it is the gift of God. (Ephesians 2:8, NKJV)

God gave us the gift of grace. There is nothing whatsoever you can do to earn this grace. God's only requirement for us to take possession of our inheritance is that we must BELIEVE. We must have faith.

That if you confess with your mouth, "Jesus is Lord," and believe in your heart that God raised him from the dead, you will be saved. For it is with your heart that you believe and are justified, and it is with your mouth that you confess and are saved. As the Scripture says, "Anyone who trusts in him will never be put to shame." (Romans 10:9-11; NKJV)

We enter the Kingdom of God through **faith**. Faith allows us to cross the bridge that Jesus Christ became for us – back into the arms of our Father. God made this available to us through His grace, but we enter into the fullness of God, as Adam and Eve experienced it in the Garden, through our faith. Our faith in the finished work of Jesus Christ becomes the foundation of our faith that we need every day:

He who did not spare his own Son, but gave him up for us all –how will he not also, along with him, graciously give us all things? (Romans 8:32, NKJV)

Neither death, nor the most humiliating form of execution was too high a price for God to pay in order to restore His relationship with us. This is why Paul asks the question, "Would He not graciously give us all things out of grace?" God has proved to us in the most public and self-sacrificing way possible, that we can trust Him with everything.

By irrevocably establishing His credibility and faithfulness, and by restoring our identity in Him, we are faced with a choice, just like Eve was, whether or not we will allow the enemy to drive us further away from our Father by listening to his lies and deception, or whether we will we trust God unconditionally and activate our faith every day to exploit the riches of His Kingdom.

When I refer to faith in the chapters that follow, it is essential to understand that the context and starting point is the cross. Our faith begins with trusting in God the Father, who did not spare His Son, Jesus Christ, and who graciously gives us good things.

In the following chapter, I write about how you get faith. The faith of Abraham, who has been called the father of faith, is described in the letter to the Romans as follows:

> *Abraham never wavered in believing God's promise. In fact, his faith grew stronger, and in this he brought glory to God. He was absolutely convinced that God is able to do anything he promised. And because of Abraham's faith, God counted him as righteous.* (Romans 4:20-22, NLT)

Abraham was absolutely convinced that God was able to fulfill what He had promised. In chapter 3, I want to show you how you can also have faith like Abraham and how to keep this faith without ever doubting the goodness of God – the God who gives you the gift of grace to turn the impossible into the possible.

3
WHY FAITH?

I'D LIKE TO START THIS CHAPTER with a testimony from my own life. I was in a situation where everything around me pointed to the fact that it would not work out and yet I still decided to believe God's Word and respond to it.

"Pastor, I don't know where you'll find your type of people, but you won't find them here ..." I remember this conversation like it was yesterday. I was a young pastor who felt really insecure when all the chaplains met with the president and campus management of the local university once a year. I was not part of the established "church group" because we weren't part of the three "sister churches" (most Afrikaans people at the time belonged to one of these three Reformed churches). We were a charismatic student church who, unlike the other churches, were not allowed a proper venue on the university campus at that time.

It was easy to determine the membership numbers of each church, because the university's admission forms had a block to check for each church denomination. Churches had certain rights based on these membership numbers. Our church, however, was not represented on the list at all. The list had one check box that included all the smaller churches and congregations that were not officially represented. This box included the Apostolic Faith Mission (a charismatic church), Baptists, as well as those who actually wanted to say, "I don't really attend church". As a result, the list that Celesté and I received from the university administration comprised a very wide spectrum. We could only visit the students who had checked the miscellaneous box on the list. We were permitted to contact them individually and invite them to attend a service. The names of students we were allowed to visit never reached more than 10% of the total first-year intake. If we were to visit someone else who had checked one of the official boxes on the form, we were accused of proselytizing.

At one of the meetings that I had attended, the University president addressed a particular issue, namely the direction that the university was taking. He spoke of a "quality university where numbers are limited to only accommodate quality students." At the time, the number of first-year enrollments was approximately 1,100 students a year, and according to the president, this number would shrink over the next few years. At this point, he looked me in the eye and said to me, **"And so, Pastor, I don't know where you'll find your type of people, but you won't find them here."** "My type of people," I thought. This meant the "misfit" list I received every year would become even smaller, because the ones on this list were not seen as "quality" students. (After this incident I would hear the phrase, "your type of people" directed at me, twice more, by some of the most influential people in the city). This incident took place around 1997/98. I cannot remember exactly what I said to the University president that day. But I did wonder why on earth I was being sent to Potchefstroom to plant a congregation that was called to transform cities. I was simply overwhelmed by what the facts and the numbers said.

I remember talking to Celesté as well as one of our church elders about this matter. This elder originally came from one of "those churches" – a charismatic church that would have been sidelined on the University list. He was not put off in the least by the growing number of negative rumors about our church and his advice to me was, "Well, then we pray 'your kind of students' into the city; we'll call them in prophetically, from the north, from the east, from the west and from the south." Truth be told, I didn't even know exactly which way north was, but we proceeded to pray together each morning as well as on Sundays. A handful of students and members of our community would prophetically "call" people in and pray specifically for more students to come to Potchefstroom. Spirit speaks to spirit - Deep calls unto deep. God honored our faith. The student numbers that were supposed to decrease, instead did the following:

- That year, there were 1,100 first-year students and a total of 4 500 full-time students at the University.
- The next year, there were 1,300 first-year students.
- Then 1,800 first-year students.
- This became 2,500 first-year students.
- Soon there were 3,500 first-year students and in subsequent years the numbers would fluctuate between 3,500 – 5,500 first-year students.
- The Potchefstroom Campus of the North-West University currently has more than 20,000 full-time

students. The University has two more campuses and between these three campuses there are more than 60,000 students. The other campuses are in Mahikeng (where we have since planted a congregation, which is led by Pastor Josephine Llale) and in Vanderbijlpark (where we are planning on planting a congregation).
The president of the University who said those things to me has since left the University. "Our type of people," on the other hand, clearly heard the call in the spirit and they came, and to this day they are still coming...
In this story, the facts and figures cried out that we were busy trying to accomplish the IMPOSSIBLE! But faith says that nothing is impossible for God – just keep on BELIEVING! Whatever impossibility you are currently struggling with – keep on BELIEVING, because with God, NOTHING is impossible. KEEP CALLING YOUR SOLUTION!

But faith says that nothing is impossible for God – just keep on BELIEVING!

For the remainder of this chapter, I would like to delve deeper into the truths of why we need faith in our lives. My family and I absolutely love to travel. I love seeing other parts of the world and learning about different cultures – there is just so much to experience! It's even more special when I can take my family with me. Our congregation is part of a wonderful spiritual family in the United States, and when we visit the various congregations in the USA from time to time, it is truly a great privilege.

I usually keep a few dollars in my safe at home so that I have some cash to get us into the USA. When I prepare for the journey, I take the banknotes out of the safe and I start eyeing the exchange rate on the Internet. How much cash do I need to take and how much money should I have available on my credit card? These are the usual questions that occupy my thoughts when I get ready to travel. Once I leave South African soil and find myself in the USA where people use another currency with its own value, my rands won't help me one bit. Even our lovely R200 note with the proud image of a leopard on it means little outside of my country. If there's no American president on the banknote, they won't accept it, even if our money is colorful and boasts beautiful images of the Big Five. Once I use the banknote with the elderly US president on it, however, I can buy any number of marvelous things – assuming I have enough of these paper presidents keeping me company. So once I get to America, I must exchange my rands for dollars because that is the only currency used for trade there. In other words, not even a whole suitcase full of rands will do me any good at all – the United States will not trade with my country's currency.

> **God's kingdom also has a "currency" – and that currency is FAITH.**

God's kingdom also has a "currency" – and that currency is FAITH. For me to live in God's kingdom, or to experience eternal life, I have to believe.

> *For God so loved the world that He gave His only begotten Son, that whoever believes in Him should not perish but have everlasting life.* (John 3:16; NKJV)

The first step in God's direction is a step of faith. By His death and resurrection, Jesus became our bridge to God. Our faith in Him enables us to take action and to cross the bridge into His Kingdom.

Paul confirms this truth in Romans 10:

> *But what does it say? "The word is near you, in your mouth and in your heart" (that is, the word of faith which we preach): that if you confess with your mouth the Lord Jesus and believe in your heart that God has raised Him from the dead, you will be saved. For with the heart one believes unto righteousness, and with the mouth confession is made unto salvation.* (Romans 10:8-10; NKJV)

In His very first sermon, Jesus began by describing faith as the door to the kingdom of God:

> *He said: "The time is fulfilled, and the kingdom of God is at hand. Repent, and believe in the gospel."* (Mark 1:15; NKJV)

The word "repent" has its roots in the Greek word 'metanoeó', which means, "to think differently." The Jews of that era were expecting a physical king, one who would save them from Roman oppression. However, then Jesus began preaching, telling them that they had to start thinking differently – that the Kingdom of this King was not a physical or temporal kingdom, but a kingdom that functions according to spiritual principles. God's kingdom is not a kingdom of a king who reigns for a particular period in history, leading one group of people into victory over another group of people. No! God's kingdom is eternal and everlasting; there will be no-one after Him. It is a kingdom for all people who share in it through their faith.

Good works do not get us into God's kingdom, nor do money or education, status, background or our bloodline. The kingdom of God and its fullness are activated in our lives once we begin thinking differently about the gospel – and when we believe it!

The power of faith emerges beautifully when a man and a woman are married. A marriage is not a spur-of-the-moment type of thing – well, not usually (unless perhaps you are in Las Vegas where this may be the case). Usually, everything begins when a young man declares his love to a young woman and promises her several things. To prove they are serious, they get engaged and this engagement usually sets many other things into motion – a church or hall must be arranged for a venue, a dress has to be made, flowers are ordered, menus are discussed and guests are invited. A motion of faith, therefore, eventually leads to a marriage and to a lifetime together as a married couple.

When we believe in our hearts, and express this belief in God with our mouths (as the young man who expresses his faith in the young woman he takes as his wife), the same significant thing usually happens. We respond to the marriage proposal of the Bridegroom, and thus we become part of God's Kingdom and in the process we are made TRULY ALIVE. Paul wrote a letter to the congregation in Rome in which he stated that he could not wait to preach the gospel in Rome, and then he said the following:

> *For I am not ashamed of the gospel of Christ, for it is the power of God to salvation for everyone who believes, for the Jew first and also for the Greek.*
> (Romans 1:16; NKJV)

This is one of Paul's most powerful statements. He explains the indisputable power of the Gospel. God proved his grace to us through His Son, Jesus Christ, so that we would not have to suffer under the yoke of slavery that sin imposed on us. So we are made free from a life without God where our destiny would be eternal death and suffering. Christ redeemed us from the power of sin and death and we are seated in heavenly places with Christ Jesus our Lord. This is the good news of the Gospel. This is the power of salvation for each one of us who believes. This good news is also meant for you. Absolutely everything it contains is yours; but you have to believe.

Paul continued by quoting from the book written by the prophet Habakkuk, when he said the following:

For in it the righteousness of God is revealed from faith to faith; as it is written, "The just shall live by faith." (Romans 1:17; NKJV)

> **What makes us just, if we are actually unjust people by nature? The answer is relatively simple – our faith.**

The just will live by faith. In chapter 2 Anita also referred to the fact that God has justified us, but what exactly does this mean? What makes us just, if we are actually unjust people by nature? The answer is relatively simple – our faith. My faith is therefore proof of my trust in another Party, that as far as my righteousness is concerned, I associate myself with someone other than myself. My righteousness is not dependent on myself, because I have been made righteous by faith in Jesus Christ.

To trust God means to REALLY begin living. A life without Jesus in the center is like having the best smart phone without a battery, or like having a luxury sports car without an engine. Every time someone responds to the good news of God and makes Jesus the central point of his or her existence, it is as if that person takes their first breath in God's life. This is why we refer to a person being born again. This is also why Paul wrote that the just - the person who confesses his or her faith in Christ - will live by faith.

Abraham understood the principle long before Jesus came to give us all Eternal Life. Abraham's faith caused him to move to a country he did not know. If you are a woman, or if you are married to one, you may well understand that Abraham most likely had to explain the situation with a fair amount of persuasion to his wife Sarai in order to get her to buy into the idea of moving. All the tents had to be taken down – and these were not the easy-to-pitch tents

To trust God means to REALLY begin living.

that we get today. It is likely that they had some type of permanent fireplace, as well as pens for their animals. Now suddenly they had to pack up everything and leave all they knew behind to journey into the unknown. "Where to, husband?" I can hear Sarai ask. To which, Abraham, unfazed, would answer, "I don't know, for God has not yet shown me the way." This is enough to upset anyone, but not Abraham. He understood God's economy. He trusted God. Abraham's faith in God meant that he was willing to sacrifice his only son, Isaac, as a burnt offering. Abraham's faith also meant that he was the Father of many, which implied that he was supposed to have MANY children, grandchildren and great-grandchildren. Finally, Abraham's faith meant that his descendants would inherit the Promised Land, because Scripture tells us:

> ***Abraham believed God, and it was accounted to him for righteousness.*** (Romans 4:3; NKJV)

Abraham received a Word from God and he believed that Word. It was his faith in God, and this faith alone, that caused God to declare him righteous and acceptable. Faith brought Abraham righteousness, which gave him a place to stand before God, as well as the right to speak. We can represent this sequence of events like this:

Abraham allowed God's Word to come close to him

His Word was a light or a revelation for Abraham

The light brought clarity or insight (Abraham could understand the revelation with his mind)

The moment when Abraham understood, he began to trust

Trust gave Abraham a place to stand

A place to stand gave Abraham a platform

Abraham had to decide if he would act or remain passive. His obedience to the Word, which brought light, caused him to take action. He took a calculated risk, because his trust was in a good and faithful God. Passivity would have meant that Abraham would procrastinate, and eventually have given up on God's promises for him.

Abraham became known as the father of faith, and we see his name frequently referred to in the New Testament. In Hebrews 11, the writer refers to Abraham when he presents the heroes of faith to us. Paul used Abraham as an example when he explains in his letter to the Romans that faith, not works, liberates us from sin. I would like to share a testimony from Renaldo (a pseudonym), who trusted and kept faith that his salary would become his tithe.

As Paul also explained to the Romans, it was not Renaldo's works that enabled him to achieve anything, but his FAITH in a good God. Renaldo's testimony has inspired thousands of people. He and his wife had been married for a few years when we met. At that point he was working with an international mining company as an engineer. What makes Renaldo's story so meaningful and significant is the fact that he responded to the Word of faith, as we have discussed above. This is the first part of his testimony:

During one of his sermons, Willem asked this question, "Is anyone here willing to trust God that their current salary will become their tithe?" Immediately, I raised my hand. I believed it would be possible, but at the time, my salary was only R3,500.00 ($350). I quickly starting working out the practical implications of this in my mind, and came to the conclusion that it would be very difficult to reach. My wife was still studying at the time, I had a scholarship that I had to pay back, and I still hadn't even factored our costs of living into the equation. In spite of my calculations, I still kept my hand up, because if my current salary were to become my tithe, it would mean that I would have to earn ten times as much. To give R3, 500.00 ($350) as a tithe, I would need to earn R35, 000.00 ($3500) – this did seem plausible as other engineers in higher positions were earning this much.

I said to myself, "You can believe that this is going to happen." It's easy enough to say that you can believe, but there are a lot of other questions that follow a decision like this. Questions like: What is faith? Why faith? How do I get faith? How do I keep faith? One last thing that went through my mind was, "Lord, I don't understand!" As a young married couple, we really struggled to make ends meet at that point in time. Apart from study debt, we had old cars that needed repairs and other debts that threatened to overwhelm us. We faced so many impossibilities and I felt guilty for not being able to provide for my wife as I felt I should. I really wanted to believe and to trust the Lord unconditionally. The Lord gave me this Word in Proverbs 3:5-6, "Trust in the Lord with all your heart, and lean not on your own understanding; In all your ways acknowledge Him, And He shall direct your paths."

I listened to the sermon series on Faith that was being preached – again and again. I was desperate, and I told the Lord, "Father, I know that Your Word says all these things, but Lord, please prove Yourself to me." I was facing a really big challenge - I had to pay my wife's final exam fees, and the payment had to be in US dollars. At that point the exchange rate was R10 to one US dollar. The exam fees had to be paid before 12pm on Wednesday. We had nothing, but the Lord came to me and asked, "Do you believe Me?" I stood there and said to Him, "Lord, Your Word says that You are our Provider, because You call into existence what we cannot even see yet – You speak the Word and it happens." We started to confess HIS WORD. Our confession was "seeing is not believing" because if we were only to believe what we saw, we would be in a lot of trouble. But we realized that once we began to believe God's Word, we would start to see His promises when we spoke these things into being. We started to confess that we would receive anonymous checks in the mail, that there would be anonymous payments made into our bank account and that angels would bring us cash in envelopes. We even said that our money would come from trees! Pastor Willem had said, "Who says money doesn't grow on trees?" Money is only paper – and paper is made from wood, and wood comes from trees! So we really confessed that money would fall from trees for us. We went really big! In the evenings I would stand on the lawn in front of our house and shout, "Money! I call you from the south and the north, from the east and from the west. Come and fill our accounts. We will buy our new house with new furniture – and we will buy it with cash, not on credit. We will have no more debt, because the Lord will cancel all our debt." We confessed, believed and trusted.

Getting back to the topic of my wife's exam fees. Wednesday came – and we still had nothing. The 12pm deadline was fast approaching. At 11:30 my broker called to say that there was a policy ready to pay out and he wanted to know into which account he should pay the money. The money not only covered the exam fees, but was even enough to fix up the cars and to pay our debt – GOD IS FAITHFUL! Money poured in, sometimes from people and sources we did not know. People from other cities sent us money via members of our Bible study group. They said that the Lord told them to sow the money into Renaldo's life. These miracles really strengthened the faith of everyone in our Bible study group. One particular person brought me money that someone else had asked him to pass on to me. This other person was a complete stranger who did not know either of us, and yet the Lord asked him to sow into my life. After everything that had to be paid had been taken care of, the money kept coming in – a river of money.

I boldly began to share this testimony with others. Every person who heard it was impacted by the Word of faith. It changed my life because I came to realize that the

Word of God is actually "easy" - you do what it says and you trust Him because He said it and He promised to fulfill it! You live it and you talk about it. Other people see it and they recognize the truth of the Good News. They begin to believe and things begin to snowball ... and in this way, we build and extend the Kingdom of God. Why? Because we are faithful to the Word of Jesus Christ.

I want to interrupt Renaldo's testimony here. You can read the second part of his testimony later on in this chapter. But for a moment, I would like to return to the other heroes of faith whose names also appear in Hebrews 11 - those men and women who walked ahead of us and cherished the expectation of serving as mentors to you and me in order to activate our faith. These men and women, like Renaldo, BELIEVED and did not depend on their own works.

"By **faith** Abel offered unto God a more excellent sacrifice than Cain" (Hebrews 11:4; feel free to read the rest of the passage in Hebrews 11). The story of Abel goes way back in time – he was the guy who called Adam and Eve "Dad" and "Mom". As far as we know, he was also the first person on earth that died. Only a sentence or two are devoted to him and yet he teaches us what it means to life by faith.

Adam and Eve must have told Abel about the time when they felt so ashamed and distant from God that they tried to make things better by covering themselves in fig leaves. Fig leaves - now that had to be very uncomfortable! Most of us know that fig leaves are hairy and cause an irritating reaction to the skin. Abel also probably heard his parents talk about God's alternative – when He slaughtered an animal, they saw blood for the first time and God covered them with the animal's skin. They probably spoke about God's standards for burnt offerings – that it always meant innocent blood would have to be shed. By **faith**, Abel then slaughtered the best of his animals and by this faith, he brought God an acceptable offering.

Enoch also had faith in God and walked closely with Him, which pleased God so much that He merely took him one day, sparing him the suffering of actual death.

At this point, while we are admiring each of these heroes of faith – almost like reading their stories on monument plaques honoring their achievements, the author of the book of Hebrews stops in order to focus our attention on the central message of these people's life stories:

> *But without faith it is impossible to please Him: for he who comes to God must believe that He is, and that He is a rewarder of those who diligently seek him.* (Hebrews 11:6; NKJV)

God is not impressed by my ideas or achievements. However, when I demonstrate faith and trust in His greatness, God is impressed. He is impressed when I believe that He exists, despite being unable to see into the future – and that He rewards those who seek Him.

Our country has 11 official languages. In our region, Setswana is one of these languages you hear a lot. In Setswana, when you ask someone how he or she is doing, the person answers with the words, *"Ke teng"* which literally

God is not impressed by my ideas or achievements. However, when I demonstrate faith and trust in His greatness, God is impressed.

means, "I am". In other words, "I'm still here, I'm not sick, I'm not dead, I'm okay." It is implied that because I am physically standing in front of you that you can see I am doing well.

In Exodus 3, we read the story of Moses and the burning bush. This was when God called him to lead the people of Israel out of Egypt and to liberate them from the yoke of slavery. Moses felt insignificant given the magnitude of this calling and could only call out to the God who was sending him. So he asked God, "Who shall I say has sent me if the Israelites ask?" This was God's answer:

> **And God said to Moses, "I AM WHO I AM." And He said, "Thus you shall say to the children of Israel, 'I AM has sent me to you.'"** (Exodus 3:14; NKJV)

"I am" refers to the essence of God's being, that He is the self-existing One, and has not been created. It also refers to the timelessness of God - the past, the present and the future become one in Him. God is unchanging and He is eternal. He is steadfast and faithful in the fulfillment of His promises. "I am" the Savior, the Prince of Peace, I am Justice, Healer, Provider. I am what I have always been. I am what I always will be and I will always be what I am today.

Before the writer of Hebrews continues to extol the heroes of faith by name, he first emphasizes that they believed wholeheartedly in the God who calls Himself "I am".

Like Abraham, Noah also received a Word from God. God gave Noah a number of very specific instructions for building an ark. The ark would provide safety for Noah, his family and every species of animal on earth once the flood came. Neither Noah nor any other person at the time had ever seen rain. Despite the frequent ridicule of others, Noah only kept one thing in mind - to act in obedience based on faith he had in God.

Sarah was another heroine of faith. As a result of her faith in God, she received power from God to bring a child into the world, despite the fact that she was very old.

The result of pure and unwavering faith in God is always action. Faith also has a ripple effect:

By **faith** that God would raise his son from death, Abraham was obedient and prepared to sacrifice Isaac as a burnt offering.

By **faith**t hat God would honor His promise to Abraham, Isaac blessed his sons.

By **faith**, Jacob blessed the sons of Joseph.

By **faith** that God would give the Promised Land to his children, Joseph asked his brothers to take his bones with them when they set out on the great exodus.

By **faith** that their children would live, Moses slaughtered the Passover Lamb and followed God's instructions carefully.

By **faith** that God would make a way through the sea, the Israelites left Egypt.

By **faith** that the God of the Israelites would save her life, Rahab hid the spies.

We are now in a better place than Abraham and all the other heroes of faith. When they sacrificed to God, every time a flame from a burnt offering went up, it carried with it a hope for a Savior to come. In our time, we have the privilege of looking back at all the things that God has promised through the years, which He has already fulfilled through His Son. We do not have to long for all the things that are yet to come, but we look back in gratitude to what has already taken place and we live in faith, in the fullness of the glory and the dominion of God.

What will people say about your faith at the end of your life?

By faith, John _____

By faith, Marianne _____

What are you trusting God to do for you? What Word did God give you, and how are you aligning your actions with that Word? Is your life story an adventure that celebrates a life of faith? I would like to share another testimony with you – a testimony filled with faith and trust in God. I will let Kobus (a pseudonym) share his story himself:

This is not my story, but His. What God has done for me, He can do for you. I grew up in a wonderful small farming community where we knew we had to live by faith, each and every day. We had to trust God for rain, trust Him for the day to day farming activities on our land, trust Him with finances, and all the other small things that others may have taken for granted. This way of life taught me to rely on God, but my faith was based on things I did for God. My perception of faith was this: the more I do for God, the more likely He would listen to my prayers and answer them.

During my first year at university, I met Willem and heard the message of faith. This opened a whole new world to me – to see what faith is really all about. Willem's words, as well as words given by others like Ron Kushmael, Daru de Wet and Ronnie Barnard, actually helped to shape my whole understanding of what faith is.

Being in Willem's company without having faith is like being a fish on dry land. If you are with him, you need to swim – there is always something greater to trust God for, because we serve a great God! We memorized the words of Hebrews 11:1 and Hebrews 11:6 by heart until the words were felt deep in our spirits. Nobody could tell me I did not have faith because we have all received a measure of faith (Rom. 12:3), but how I would live my faith was up to me.

To me, faith was like a jigsaw puzzle. With a few pieces, I would only have a partial picture and partial results. I had to find the pieces of the puzzle for myself, so that I could get the whole picture of what faith was – so that I could trust wholeheartedly. Puzzle pieces such as "we receive through grace and not works" (Eph. 2:8), "our words have power when we speak" (Jer. 5:14) and "faith is not a formula but a relationship, to know the One in whom we have faith" (2 Tim 1:12). However, I also came to understand that every person's puzzle is different, and therefore Jesus said: "As with YOUR faith it will be to you"... each person has to find his or her own pieces of the puzzle in their relationship with God.

I began to apply the Word of God in every sphere of my life. I was faced with so many impossible situations but I trusted the Father that, through His Word, I would be able to speak into existence all that I needed. I was still a student when I began trusting God for my first breakthrough, which was paying my rent. Honestly, I had no idea how I was going to pay. I simply stood before God and began to apply His living Word. That night someone – I still don't know who – threw an envelope full of money through my window. It was the exact amount that I had needed. That year, I also went on a missions trip to a country in the Middle East, together with a group of students. This is where my faith was really tested for the first time. We still needed the money to pay for one flight when we arrived at the airport. One of the people who came to say goodbye to us sowed an amount that covered part of the cost of the flight. We went to the airport chapel with this money and prayed over it. We recounted it, but it still wasn't enough. We prayed over it again, and it was now the exact amount *that we needed! God had increased the money in His supernatural way! Years later I found out that God did not want us to live from miracle to miracle, but instead that we should simply live by faith on a daily basis. This did not mean, however, that I would never again face the impossible.*

I wanted to get married at that point in my life, but needed money for the ring, renting a good suit and paying for the honeymoon. I also needed a general increase in my monthly income. I wrote down these needs and every morning I prayed God's Word over them. God fulfilled each and every one of these needs. The last of the money I needed for the honeymoon came on the day we left, but God was never late.

As I began to trust God for small things, my faith became stronger – like muscles you exercise regularly. We began to trust God for bigger things – and as the impossible challenges grew bigger, our faith in God grew as well. After our wedding, my wife and I had to go to a conference in the USA and we needed R30, 000 ($3000) for this trip. A year later, we had to go for training (again in the USA) for which we needed R100, 000 ($10 000). We were also trusting God for things like health, relationships and souls on the university campus. Each time I would write down the impossible challenge and then pray over it during my personal devotion time. Writing down what I needed and praying over these with the Word was not a way of trying to twist God's arm, but it was a way of hearing the Word of God repeatedly - for myself, from myself. This built my faith muscle so that I could trust God more confidently. All we had was God and His Word. God came through in each and every one of our needs because *it is His Father's heart to provide.*

I used to be driven by a combination of fear and good works, until God and His Word became alive to me. I began to understand that my words have power – we read in Hebrews 11:3 that the Words of God created everything; and hence I also have the ability to create with God's Word. We have been living by faith ever since. It keeps us close to God, dependent on Him, and it builds our relationship with Him. Never stand back for less than you have been called to do. The just shall live by faith and each one has received a measure of faith – the size of a mustard seed. Every mountain of impossibility that stands before you simply has to move.

Wow, what a testimony! Yet so often in our lives, although we really believe that Jesus Christ died for us and we are saved through faith, it is here as we enter God's kingdom that our faith often leaves us. We try and function in the kingdom of God according to the standards and principles of the world we live in, relying on our own good works (like Kobus used to believe). This is like trying to buy something in a foreign country using your own local currency, or like competing in a golf tournament with a soccer ball. The only way we can function in the kingdom of God is by faith.

False preachers were evident in the congregation of the Galatians - they tried to teach that faith was not sufficient in the kingdom of God. There were rumors that people were still obliged to do good deeds in order to be acceptable before God. Let's take a look at how Paul dealt with this situation in his role as apostle and father of the congregation.

O foolish Galatians! Who has bewitched you that you should not obey the truth, before whose eyes

Jesus Christ was clearly portrayed among you as crucified? This only I want to learn from you: Did you receive the Spirit by the works of the law, or by the hearing of faith? Are you so foolish? Having begun in the Spirit, are you now being made perfect by the flesh? (Galatians 3:1-3; NKJV)

I've been to many congregations in South Africa as well as in the USA, and I can assure you that no preacher talks to his congregation like this. I have to confess, I was quite stunned when I read Paul's choice of words in reaction to these people. However, I understood why Paul addressed the matter so firmly. Everything we receive from God, we receive by faith. We are born again by faith, and from that day onwards we function within God's kingdom, by faith. The enemy uses subtle means to cloud the truth, which is why Paul had to be firm. Paul is saying that we should not be foolish – starting out in faith and then thinking that our own actions could take us further than God Himself could have taken us.

The currency of God's Kingdom is faith!

The currency of God's Kingdom is faith! Only faith in God's finished work gives us access to Him and His Kingdom. Faith alone makes it possible for us to be ambassadors who can make the full extent and governance of His Kingdom felt in our homes and our communities. When the sons of God stand up in faith, the world no longer has to wait with eager expectation for the sons of God to be revealed (Rom 8:19) but can experience the impact they make in the world around them with joy and relief!

After having read everything in this chapter so far, you might still be wondering, "Why faith? What are the benefits of faith and

Why Faith?

what does faith hold for me?" I would, therefore, like to conclude this chapter by referring to eight things that faith can do for you, or mean to you.

Faith determines what God can DO in my life

In Matthew 9:29 we read:

> *"According to your faith let it be to you"* (Matthew 9:29, NKJV)

Here God says, "*You* can choose how many blessings you want to experience in your life. You can choose the number of prayers you would like to have answered. *You* can choose the extent to which you want Me to work in your life. These choices are all made *based on your faith.*" There are more than 7,000 promises in the Bible. Faith is the key that unlocks these promises. Faith determines what God can do in your life and how much of it He can do!

The power of faith does not exist so that you can "get more things." What I believe, and I will say this throughout this book, is that God will bless you based on your obedience, to be a blessing to others - a blessing to your family, to the people who work with you, to your city and also to your country. This book is not intended to convince you that God's economy is aimed at giving you a greater sense of material comfort. Instead, I believe that His plan is for the earth and its people to turn to Him.

The power of faith does not exist so that you can "get more things".

In South Africa, we are confronted with the most extreme poverty, often on a daily basis. We see the abuse and corruption around us, and the impact of violence on our people. For this very reason, in the midst of this broken world, we stand firm with the Word of righteousness and we believe in God's absolute goodness. We believe that the impossible will have to bow down before our God who can turn the impossible into the possible.

Do you remember Renaldo's testimony? He was the one who responded to the challenge of having his current income become his tithe. Here is the rest of his testimony:

I was the one who raised my hand and said that I believed my current income would become my tithe. According to my calculations, this would only have been possible over four years, but three and a half months later, I was able to tithe an amount of R3, 500 ($350). How did my income grow to R35, 000 ($3500)? I had four salary increases and promotions in three and a half months. This was truly a miracle. All I did was respond to the Word.

The mining company that I worked for had a policy that insisted my family and I had to move to a larger house every time I got promoted. Each time we had to move, I received a special allowance. These allowances were so large that by the time we moved for the fourth time we could afford to leave all the furniture behind in our old house for the workers at the transport company to keep for themselves. We bought brand new furniture for our new house. All of this started with a confession and with believing in God and the truth of His Word. I asked Willem to extend this invitation for a second time – to invite people to trust God again that their salaries would become their tithes.

A few years later I left the company and started my own firm with contracts in Africa. My income while at the international mining company then became my tithe (again), and my income kept growing. God gave us the opportunity to speak to people across the world, telling them to trust God and His Word more than anything.

Faith can SOLVE impossible problems

You may feel as if you are facing impossible problems right now. Things may feel too big to overcome, and you may feel as if they are getting the better of you. Read with me what is written in Matthew 17:20:

> **So Jesus said to them, "Because of your unbelief; for assuredly, I say to you, if you have faith as a mustard seed, you will say to this mountain, 'Move from here to there,' and it will move; and nothing will be impossible for you.** (Matthew 17:20, NKJV)

When you are faced with an impossible situation, you need to keep this promise close to you. You don't need a LOT of faith. You can take your small amount of faith and put it into the hands of a HUGE God, and the results will also be GREATLY POSITIVE.

Faith is the key to ANSWERED prayer

So often, people's prayers sound something like this: "Honorable Sir, if You are not too busy and if You can afford to, can you please consider attending to what I am asking of You?" However, in Matthew 21:22 we read the following:

> **"And whatever things you ask in prayer, believing, you will receive"** (Matthew 21:22, NKJV)

The Bible tells us, "If you believe that you have already received it, then you will receive it." This means that before the fact, you have to believe that your prayer has been answered. Your faith is the key to answered prayer.

Faith is the secret to SUCCESS

We read in Mark 9 that Jesus tells the father of the child tormented by evil spirits the following:

> ... *all things are possible to him who believes.* (Mark 9:23, NKJV)

Is this true? Yes, of course it's true, because faith changes dreams into reality. Faith gives you the guts to move ahead. To set a goal is to declare your faith. Warner von Braun, the man who initiated the space age, and the first person to introduce rockets to the USA once said: "Not a single great achievement in history happened without faith." Faith is the secret to success. "*All things* are possible for him who believes."

Faith is the foundation of MIRACLES

> "*Most assuredly, I say to you, he who believes in Me, the works that I do he will do also; and greater works than these he will do, because I go to My Father*" (John 14:12, NKJV)

This is one of the most amazing things that Jesus ever said. Do you do greater things than Jesus? I don't even achieve a fraction of what Jesus did, and yet these words that He spoke are true. Why? At the time when Jesus walked the earth, miracles were limited to the place where He was at a particular time. However, when Christians pray today, whether they are alone or together corporately, miracles can happen anywhere across the globe. Actually, miracles can happen in many places at the same time, because Christians already BELIEVE that their prayers have been answered. The question is, does God still perform miracles today? Of course He does! He does it through people and prayer. Faith is the foundation of miracles!

The Bible teaches that a lack of faith is SIN

... for whatever is not from faith is sin. (Romans 14:23, NKJV)

It is clear that whatever is not born out of faith is sin. God expects us to depend on Him, and Him alone.

Faith is how we PLEASE God

Don't you love it when your kids trust you completely? Perhaps you don't have children, but you probably remember how happy your parents were when you trusted them. We read these words in Hebrews 11:6:

But without faith it is impossible to please Him, for he who comes to God must believe that He is, and that He is a rewarder of those who diligently seek Him. (Hebrews 11:6, NKJV)

God is overjoyed when His children place their trust in Him. Your faith gives Him immense pleasure.

Faith enables you to maintain a SUCCESSFUL lifestyle

In 1 John 5:4 we read:

For whatever is born of God overcomes the world.

And this is the victory that has overcome the world
- our faith. (1 John 5:4, NKJV)

Faith gives us self-confidence. Faith cancels out fear. Faith gives you the ability to press on and stick it out. Imagine for a moment, Moses and Aaron standing at the Red Sea as it opens. Moses turns to Aaron and says, "You go first ", but Aaron replies, "Oh no! Ladies first!" Faith gives you the ability to have sufficient self-confidence to move ahead and achieve success in life.

These are the qualities of Kingdom faith:
- Kingdom faith is steadfast and unwavering even during the storms of life.
- Kingdom faith is founded on God's encompassing Wisdom and Knowledge, not on our limited knowledge.
- Kingdom faith is larger than our human insight.
- Kingdom faith is purified by testing.
- Kingdom faith is rewarded after it has been tested.
- Kingdom faith is rewarded by the King Himself.
- Kingdom faith is given and sustained by the King.
- Kingdom faith is not afraid of trials.
- Kingdom faith surrenders the future into God's hands.

The title of this chapter is, "Why Faith?" My prayer is that I have been able to give you the answer, not only from the Word of God but also from people's testimonies. If you still feel the slightest bit of doubt in your heart, I would like to offer Albert's testimony in conclusion. His story will be proof that the key to God's Kingdom is FAITH:

My first great test of faith came after I had graduated from university and began to work with a large mining firm.

The department where I had been placed worked with tenders and I had to compile the tender contracts. Some of these contracts stretched over a few hundred pages – it seemed like endless pages to me – and everything was in English. My first language is Afrikaans and English has never been my strong suit. I was facing a huge challenge. My manager's first language was English, and he was a linguistic perfectionist to boot. He gave me a really hard time in the beginning. However, I kept blessing him and confessed Psalm 112, "that God would lift me up and honor me before men". As I look back at these times, I am able to laugh, but at that stage it felt like I was facing the impossible. English was utterly foreign to me. I had a choice – would I allow myself to be overwhelmed by the complexity of my work situation, or would I simply do everything that I could to get the job done? I surrounded myself with God's Word, immersing myself in the Word and confessing it over my life. The Lord gave me His supernatural grace and favor. He gave me the ability to understand and compile the contracts so well, to the extent that my manager and I became good friends! I was trusted to look after his house when he and his family went away on vacation, and he was instrumental in my future promotions at work.

Since I was a child I've had a dream that seemed larger than a mountain, but it burnt in my heart like a flame. I've always dreamt that I would be in a position to help people to make sound and wise decisions about finances and investments. I knew that one day I would get to live out this dream. I was fortunate enough to be part of a church congregation where we would be challenged to live out our dreams – and in the process to take the leap of faith and to leave the rest to God. Trust God to honor His Word and dare to walk the walk with Him. At that point in my life, I was thirty years old and already in a senior management position, but I urgently felt that it was time to take the leap of faith. I just knew deep inside me that I had to start my own business. I quit my job and joined an independent broker firm where I worked purely for commission, without the luxury of a steady salary. I actually prefer stability and this decision was the exact opposite. On the other hand, it was also the beginning of a wonderful journey of faith – to get out of the security of a fixed income and to begin to trust God for everything.

Although I have to admit that it was really hard in the beginning, the Lord never disappointed me and clients came to me in supernatural ways. Time and time again I was stunned to hear that people I did not even know had referred clients to me. Today I am one of a small group of brokers in my country to have a category two license, which means that I can act as a fund manager. This is living proof of the fact that you can take God at His Word and dare to walk the walk with Him. His Word will never come back unfulfilled, and He will never let you down.

Every time when I have had to make serious decisions regarding my career, I have been confronted with the practical implications of my dream, and with the realities surrounding me. Also, people would often look at me in the physical realm and discourage me from taking a leap of faith and living my dream. "Don't be conformed to this world, always dragging you down..." So often those closest to me were the most negative of all, and often they were the ones who discouraged me. But fortunately, I believe that you have to surround yourself with a community of faithful believers. I found that the Word that I had heard from Willem week after week, together with the encouragement of my faith-friends, gave me the strength to think beyond the limitations of my own little world and to show the impossible who is in charge. Christ Jesus and His Word are the master contractors in my life. Based on the Word that I had drawn nearer to, I believe in taking calculated risks. I took a few daring steps, but I took care that my vessels were large enough for God to provide in a supernatural way (I'm indirectly referencing Elijah and the widow who borrowed vessels in order to receive oil in 2 Kings 4:7). The secret is not to chase after money in life, but to live your dream and your passion – money will come by itself!

4
THE SEED OF FAITH

WHENEVER WE TALK ABOUT THE ORIGIN OF FAITH, we use the metaphor of a seed. Everything in life begins with a seed. Let's use the example of an orange tree. Various parts of our country are decorated with bright orange splashes of large orange groves, especially in the early winter. South Africa's multi-national fruit industry all started with those small, hard, white things that get stuck between your teeth when you bite into a juicy orange. When a seed is planted in the soil, a God-given process is set in motion: the seed bursts open and roots and stems begin to grow out of it; as if the seed had a built-in thermometer and hydrometer to determine the exact moment to start growing. The power within the seed has been programmed in such a way that it has an intense desire to grow – that even the heavy layer of soil on top of the seed cannot deter from breaking through and meeting the sunlight. The seed of an orange can seem small and insignificant, but it contains within itself all the genetic materials needed to produce a tree, with new fruits and seeds of its own – and those seeds all carry within themselves enough potential to produce a whole grove of orange trees.

Everything in life begins with a seed.

There is even *more* potential contained within a human seed. When two gametes (cells that are too small to be visible to the naked eye, loaded with enough genetic material to give life to a new person) are joined, this new life, or human being has the capacity to give life to the next generation as well. People usually recognize the potential of a growing (human) seed. They immediately rush to the store and buy things like baby clothes, diapers and toys for the new baby. When we welcome the new baby into our midst, we are keenly aware of the fact that the baby will not remain a baby forever. They might be lying in the stroller wrapped in soft blankets *now*, but he or she will grow up and have the full potential to go to school, get married and raise children of their own. We look at this new baby and know that locked within their being is the potential to have an intimate and personal relationship with God, make an impact for His kingdom and influence various spheres of society through his or her unique gifts and talents.

> **However small a seed may be, the potential it contains is unimaginably big.**

However small a seed may be, the potential it contains is unimaginably big. With this in mind you can understand why God said to Zechariah,

For who has despised the day of small things?
(Zechariah 4:10; NKJV)

There have been countless major businesses, paintings, films, and patents that have revolutionized the way we live, think, and go about our daily lives. All of them came into being from a simple idea or concept. The process usually unfolds as follows: You have an idea (seed), which when fertilized, germinates into a thought.

The thought, in turn, germinates into a concept and concepts are the basic material for dreams and visions. When something is invented, we call it the "brain child" of the inventor – it started as a seed, but has developed to maturity.

When somebody shares an idea with friends or family at a social gathering, it's often laughed at or dismissed as wishful thinking. I wonder how many good ideas were crushed in careless conversations. How many dreams and concepts have died by the hands (or words) of people closest to us? Do not underestimate the day of small beginnings – it might only be an idea, a concept or a thought, but that small seed has the potential to grow into something magnificent.

It might only be an idea, a concept or a thought, but that small seed has the potential to grow into something magnificent.

A seed looks tiny and insignificant, but within the right environment of fertile soil, light and water, it can grow into something big and meaningful, which is perhaps the reason God compares our faith with a seed: the mustard seed.

> *... for assuredly, I say to you, if you have faith as a mustard seed, you will say to this mountain, 'Move from here to there,' and it will move; and nothing will be impossible for you.* (Matthew 17:20, NKJV)

I always thought, "If only I could have faith like a mustard seed." I thought if I concentrated hard enough and mentally focused on it, I could produce faith like a mustard seed. However, when I started searching the scriptures and asking questions (I mean, why a mustard seed? Why not a bigger seed?), I began to understand that believing is seeing. Jesus referred to this mustard seed faith after his disciples had prayed for a child to be healed. They were overwhelmed by the child's grotesque injuries from falling into boiling water and into fires. The child was probably covered with burns and boils, which is probably why the disciples had a hard time praying. They saw the scars and wounds, but they completely ignored the One who could heal the child – read this section with me:

> *"And when they had come to the multitude, a man came to Him, kneeling down to Him and saying, "Lord, have mercy on my son, for he is an epileptic and suffers severely; for he often falls into the fire and often into the water. So I brought him to Your disciples, but they could not cure him."*
>
> *Then Jesus answered and said, "O faithless and perverse generation, how long shall I be with you? How long shall I bear with you? Bring him here to Me." And Jesus rebuked the demon, and it came out of him; and the child was cured from that very hour. Then the disciples came to Jesus privately and said, "Why could we not cast it out?"*
>
> *So Jesus said to them, "Because of your unbelief; for assuredly, I say to you, if you have faith as a mustard seed, you will say to this mountain, 'Move from here to there,' and it will move; and nothing will be impossible for you.* (Matthew 17:14-20 NKJV)

In verse 17, Jesus rebuked his disciples, because they'd been around Him for such a long time, and yet, they still didn't understand how His ministry worked. In this verse Jesus describes them as faithless and perverse. This is bad – you almost feel sorry for them, but it's important that you and I understand that God **expects** us to live by faith and through faith.

Jesus helped them understand that seeing is NOT believing, that faith means being able to see as God sees. It was after this scenario that He used the metaphor of the mustard seed. As we'll discuss later on, mustard is described as something that will make your eyes water and your tongue burn. When you have faith like a mustard seed, YOU will TELL the IMPOSSIBILITY to "move!" Your focus is no longer on the mountain, but on the direction you will see the mountain move to.

Not only is the mustard seed compared with faith, but in Mark 4, it is also described as follows:

> *Then He said, "To what shall we liken the kingdom of God? Or with what parable shall we picture it? It is like a mustard seed which, when it is sown on the ground, is smaller than all the seeds on earth; but when it is sown, it grows up and becomes greater than all herbs, and shoots out large branches, so that the birds of the air may nest under its shade."* (Mark 4:30-32, NKJV)

The mustard seed is described as the smallest of all the seeds, and yet it grows to be bigger than all of the other herb plants and

> **When you have faith like a mustard seed, YOU will TELL the IMPOSSIBILITY to "move!" Your focus is no longer on the mountain, but on the direction you will see the mountain move to.**

eventually shoots out large branches. This section in Mark, together with the previous section in Matthew, really spoke to me. I will discuss the scientific significance of this scripture in a moment, but it's amazing to experience God's greatness in this passage of scripture in that Jesus not only spoke as a carpenter, but as one who displayed a great amount of insight into the properties of the mustard seed. He describes the mustard seed here as a Kingdom seed. This scripture convinced me that the Kingdom of God also begins with a seed. We can sow spiritual seed into our cities through prayer and good works, and see the impact of that seed in the growth of our cities - the economy and even the physical fruitfulness of our land will reflect the greatness of God.

Why the mustard seed? I did some research into the scientific properties of the mustard plant and would like to share some interesting facts with you.

The mustard plant is described as a fibrous, annual plant that grows to an average height of one meter. Research shows, however,

that these plants can reach a height of up to four meters in Israel. Mustard plants are specifically planted for their fragrant seeds and leaves.

As most of us learned in science or biology class in school, living organisms are classified into different groups. All plants, for example, belong to a specific group. Plants that share certain characteristics are sub-divided into further sections, and within these sections, plants are divided into classes. Classes become orders, orders families, and families become genera. Within genera we find different individual species. The scientific classification of the mustard plant looks like this:

Kingdom: Plantae
Phylum: Magnoliophyta
Class: Magnoliopsida
Order: Brassicales
Family: Brassicaceae (Crusifereae)
Genus: Brassica

Perhaps you're wondering why I am going the scientific route here. I'm quite sure you didn't buy this book to get a taxonomy lesson, but when you look at the classification of the mustard plant, something very interesting emerges. In the mustard plant's family, there are various other kinds of vegetables, for example: radishes, broccoli, cauliflower, cabbage, Brussels sprouts and Chinese cabbage. Even though mustard is grouped with these various types of vegetables, it is actually described as an herb or spice. Herbs differ from vegetables in the sense that they are used in small amounts to give flavor to food rather than being a form of food in itself. The flowering structure of this diverse family is very interesting. The petals of the flowers are arranged across from each other; it looks like a cross, and this is where the alternate family name, *Cruciferae* (cruciform) comes from.

The family *Brassicaceae / Cruciferae*, also known (in English) as the mustard or cabbage family, constitutes a large part of the world's winter vegetables. Even though the mustard plant dies in the winter, this is the season that the seedpods ripen, become dry enough to be harvested, and yield new mustard seeds, and naturally a new range of products on the market.

A mustard seed is tiny – about one-fifteenth of an inch in

diameter – and yet, despite its size, it has the ability to burn your mouth rather severely, which isn't something you would usually expect from a *tiny* seed. There are many products that come from mustard seeds, but the most well-known one is the yellow-brown paste we called "mustard" that we use to add flavor to our food. Strong mustard usually causes your eyes to water and creates a hot sensation on the roof of your mouth. I'm sure most of you have experienced this sensation, especially if you've put too much mustard on a hotdog or burger.

Having said this, there are a few interesting parallels between mustard plants and faith. Firstly, the mustard plant is described as the one plant in the *Brassica* family that is totally different from the rest of its radish and cabbage family. In fact, the strong flavor and taste are the only shared qualities between the mustard plant and its family. The same can be said about people who trust God unconditionally and who begin to live in the gift of grace that was given to us in Christ, as opposed to those who don't.

Now thanks be to God who always leads us in triumph in Christ, and through us diffuses the fragrance of His knowledge in every place. For we are to God the fragrance of Christ among those who are being saved and among those who are perishing" (2 Corinthians 2:14-15, NKJV)

When you and I begin to live by faith, in other words we accept what God did for us through Christ, and we begin to live each day trusting God unconditionally, it distinguishes us from the people around us. It's considered normal to live according to the philosophy of "seeing-is-believing", where our thoughts, words and actions are dictated to by our natural or physical environment. When we live by faith, however, we differ from the status quo because we begin to elevate God's Word and character above all else.

I have already mentioned that the flower petals of the mustard plant are arranged in the shape of a cross. The flowers are later pollinated and then grow into long pods, which securely protect the valuable mustard seeds inside it. Faith works in the same way. Isn't it true that the faith Jesus speaks of in Matthew also emanates from the cross? Our faith is grounded in God, who kept His Word and whose Word did not return empty or void to Him in Christ. In Christ, God kept every promise, and confirmed His Word. As the Holy Spirit reveals this truth to us, a valuable mustard seed-like faith is formed and germinates in our hearts. It is the revelation of the cross that enables us to live by faith, in the reality of the unseen, and no longer according to the flesh or what we can physically see.

> **When we live by faith, however, we differ from the status quo because we begin to elevate God's Word and character above all else.**

Another interesting point is that the *Brassica* family bears fruit in the winter, becoming a good source of food. The mustard seed only matures during the fall and winter months. The seed yields many useful products, but more than that, the seed, in itself, holds a promise and an expectation for the future in the following season. This is very often also the case when it comes to faith. In times when there does not seem to be much life or progress in our environment or our lives, faith emerges. When we've run out of plans and when we have reached the end of our rope, that's when our faith in a God, for whom nothing is impossible, emerges again and reminds us of the fullness we have in Christ Jesus. This happens when everything around us appears dead and lifeless. It is in these dry seasons that the seed of faith, the promise of new life, will begin to create hope in the midst of our circumstances.

Mustard is a yellow or brownish paste that can cause the tongue to burn and the eyes to water, especially if eaten in excess. This is exactly what faith does to us. When we begin to act according to our faith, it has an effect on the tongue – on our words, and the way we talk in the midst of situations. Faith causes my eyes to water, resulting in the stark reality of life's circumstances to fade and blur, causing me to see those things with eyes of faith. Paul said in his letter to the Corinthians that "we walk by faith and not by sight". Faith, a firm belief in what God has said or revealed to me, causes me to speak and act as if the unseen, the picture of faith, becomes a bigger reality than what I can see, hear or experience in the visible realm.

In all the similarities between the mustard plant and our faith, I think the main reason why Jesus compared faith with a mustard seed is because it is such a tiny seed. The tiny, one-fifteenth of an inch seed contains all the potential and all that is needed to grow into a fully developed mustard plant, in all its glory. Faith contains the same qualities – it may be as small as a mustard seed, but it contains the potential for each of us to fully operate in the realm of the spirit, just like Jesus demonstrated for us when He was on earth. Faith, as small as a mustard seed, moves mountains, turns the invisible into the visible, and makes heaven a tangible reality on earth.

Each of us has received a seed of faith, like a mustard seed. And each of us has received the measure of faith to respond to what Jesus did for us on the cross and become born again. This is the same faith that enables us to move mountains and to establish the kingdom of God on earth. Andrew Wommack writes the following in his article '*The Faith of God*':

> *When we hear God's Word, the Holy Spirit empowers it, and if we receive the truth, God's supernatural faith enters us. We were so destitute that we couldn't even believe the good news on our own. God had to make His kind of faith available to us so that we could believe in Him and receive His salvation. We were saved by using God's supernatural faith to receive His grace.*

In Romans 12:3 Paul states that each person has received a measure of faith:

> **For I say, through the grace given to me, to everyone who is among you, not to think of himself more highly than he ought to think, but to think soberly, as God has dealt to each one a measure of faith.** (Romans 12:3, NKJV)

The King James Version refers to '**the** measure of faith.' In other words, people did not receive different measures of faith, but the same measure of faith. Paul, in turn, says that he died in himself and that he lived his life with the same faith Jesus had.

> **I have been crucified with Christ; it is no longer I who live, but Christ lives in me; and the life which I now live in the flesh I live by faith in the Son**

of God, who loved me and gave Himself for me.
(Galatians 2:20, NKJV)

The original Greek word used in this passage is *tou*, which means 'of the'. In other words, the Scripture should read as follows: *and the life which I now live in the flesh I live by faith **of the** Son of God.* What Paul means is that he lived his life with God's faith – the same faith Jesus had when He was on earth. After all, Jesus said in John 14:12, that:

Most assuredly, I say to you, he who believes in Me, the works that I do he will do also; and greater works than these he will do, because I go to My Father. (NKJV)

The seed of faith that God has placed inside us empowers us to do what Jesus did, and even more! Peter wrote about the seed of faith we received at the very beginning of his second Epistle and states that we received the same measure of faith as all the heroes of faith that have gone before us.

Simon Peter, a bondservant and apostle of Jesus Christ, To those who have obtained like precious faith with us by the righteousness of our God and Savior Jesus Christ. (2 Peter 1:1, NKJV)

When 'like precious faith' is translated directly from the Greek, it means 'faith of equal value'. Peter said that the measure of faith we received has the same value as the faith he had received. We have received the same faith that made Peter boldly stand up on the day of Pentecost and preach the first sermon of the New Testament church, as we know it today to a huge crowd of people. Our faith is equal in value to Peter's faith – his faith that healed so many people, that the sick were even carried outside on stretchers, in the hope that Peter's shadow would fall on them and heal them.

I'd like to share Bernard's testimony with you. This is a testimony that speaks of faith – an unshakeable faith in God that changed the impossible into the possible:

During my student years, I worked at the Clover Dairy Company during vacations. This was the company where my father worked, and I worked there to help pay for my studies. My salary was R25 (about $2,50) a day – and during that time I saw that it was much better to buy and sell than to carry around heavy crates like a laborer. I saw an opportunity to enter the world of marketing, and specifically the world of marketing and promoting clothing. I took R100 (about $10) and bought my first 30 T-shirts at R3 (about 30c) a shirt that I then sold at a profit. One thing led to another and this $10 ultimately became a business that was far bigger than any of us could have imagined. I then asked Erika, my girlfriend (now my precious wife), to think of a name for the business. We are totally convinced that the name she came up with was divinely inspired – the name of the business is No Limits. God says in His Word that nothing is impossible. No Limits is a road of faith we have walked, a story of faith that has given rise to thousands of testimonies. I would like to share two of them with you here.

As the business grew, I became more and more involved in the management of the business, but I did not want to be office-bound all the time. I therefore decided to visit some of our key clients. Our clients included, among others, universities in South Africa, corporate clients and schools. In order to escape from the office, I decided to visit the North-West University, specifically the Potchefstroom Campus to negotiate with the dormitories (or student residences). Erika and I had always wanted to move to a more rural environment, although a step in that direction did not seem practical in terms of a business decision. After all, I was supposed to be the "main peanut" in the packet, and it would not make sense to come and live in a "small place" like Potchefstroom. As the years passed, doors started opening and we got the opportunity to pitch a business plan for a small space on the Potchefstroom Campus (all interested parties were given the opportunity to present their plans). This was a rare opportunity, so we grabbed it with both hands. At the time (in 2004), the book of Joshua meant a great deal to me, and certain passages really spoke to me. Joshua 1:5 says:

No man shall be able to stand before you all the days of your life; as I was with Moses, so I will be with you. I will not leave you nor forsake you. (NKJV)

Joshua 1:9 says:

Have I not commanded you? Be strong and of good courage; do not be afraid, nor be dismayed, for the LORD your God is with you wherever you go. (NKJV)

On the day we delivered our presentation to the University, they opened the meeting by reading Joshua 1:5. The presentation was done in the Council Chamber, and the moment they opened the proceedings with Scripture reading, I knew something great was about to happen. There were a number of other large companies at the meeting who were competing for the same space on campus as we were, but by God's grace and favor, we were awarded the business. We signed the contract and I told all of our employees throughout 2004 that we were going to be moving to Potchefstroom. I put my house on the market and we thought we were on our way, however I still struggled to make sense of everything.

In January 2005, we returned from vacation and needed to open the offices and the store in Potchefstroom. The store was ready, but I still did not feel convinced that we should actually move towns. On the one hand my head told me to move, but on the other hand my heart would not quite believe it. Our daughter, Zinandi, was due to start Grade R (first year of primary school) on the 12th January 2005 and we did not want to put her in a new school, only to remove her a few weeks later and then have to put her in another new school in a new town. Our time was running out. We had to decide where we wanted to be for the next season in our lives. On the 8th of January 2005, during my devotions, I said to the Lord: "Lord, we don't have a lot of time, we need to know where we are going." The Holy Spirit led me to Joshua 1:11 and I read:

Pass through the camp and command the people, saying, 'Prepare provisions for yourselves, for within three days you will cross over this Jordan, to go in to possess the land which the LORD your God is giving you to possess. (NKJV)

It was very clear to me that the Lord was using Scripture to tell me that we had to move. It still didn't make complete business sense for me, however, to move to a smaller town – after all, everybody knows that Gauteng Province is where the money is and a business is only viable if you make more money than you spend. I remained silent and said nothing to Erika about God's answer to me. The next morning I told the Lord that He had given me a good answer, just not the answer I had in mind. The Lord, in His grace and love, told me to read Joshua 1:9 – a passage that I knew very well. It says:

Be strong and of good courage; do not be afraid, nor be dismayed, for the LORD your God is with you wherever you go. (NKJV)

I decided there and then that I would move - by faith and obedience. After all, God told me He would be with me wherever I went. He was sending us to Potchefstroom even though it did not make sense to me. That same afternoon someone from Potchefstroom, who hadn't known anything about the questions and uncertainties I was battling with, sent me a message, reminding me of Joshua 1:11– the section where God told Joshua to prepare the people to move because they were going to cross the river Jordan and take possession of the land in three days. The same person also sent me a scripture from Deuteronomy, saying something similar:

Prepare provisions for yourselves, for within three days you will cross over this Jordan, to go in to possess the land which the LORD your God is

giving you to possess. (NKJV)

That afternoon, when I switched on the TV, there happened to be a documentary about the life of Joshua. I saw the image of Joshua sending the ark of the Lord ahead of them, and how the ark stopped the powerful flow of water in the river, enabling them to cross on dry ground.

The Lord made it clear to me that we needed to move to Potchefstroom – He spoke through the Word, through people and through a television program. I simply told Erika that we had to move. We packed our bags and moved to Potchefstroom - with nothing more than our bags. We did not have accommodation, our house had not yet been sold, but we saw one miracle after another take place. The first call I received when we entered Potchefstroom came from Hans Weyers, from "Potchefstroom Gimnasium" High School. He didn't know me from a bar of soap but said that they wanted to place an order with my business. It was as if God wanted to make it clear that we didn't need to worry about finances at all, because if He sent me, there would always be provision. God provided for us time and time again. We opened the North-West University campus store, and as a result of the business that we were able to generate there, the University of Johannesburg came to inspect our business model. This led to us being able to open a campus store at the University of Johannesburg. The same thing happened with the University of Pretoria and various other business opportunities followed after that.

I would like to interrupt Bernard's testimony for a moment, and point out that the steps he took were an act of faith. His faith in

God determined what his actions would be – in realistic terms a move to Potchefstroom did not make sense, but Bernard decided not to be realistic and instead he acted out in faith by believing in God's plan for him and his family. Let's continue reading Bernard's testimony, picking up from where he decided to be obedient to the will of God while everybody was telling him that this was not the way to do things:

The University of Johannesburg gave us the opportunity to tender for their campus store. Ten companies from across South Africa were invited, as well as major international companies such as Canterbury, Adidas and Wilson. It felt to me like all the world's big brands were there, and then there was us - No Limits, the smallest of all the companies there. Just before the tender process started, God began speaking to me – I had all these plans going through my head of what we needed to do to expand – we would need to open up branches and have representatives across the whole of Southern Africa. One of the legs that we would need to focus on would be universities and campuses, in other words opening campus stores. I knew everything about what we had to do, but I had no clue how to do it. Once again, God spoke to me by reminding me of a series of sermons preached by Pastor Willem Nel. The series called 'Unlimited God' encouraged us to never limit God. Through this series, God said to me: "Bernard, you know what to do, leave the 'how to' part to Me, I'll take care of it." The University of Johannesburg ended up choosing my business to tender for the campus store.

At the exact same time we were asked to tender for the store, Gerrit, my brother, who is also a partner in our business, received a letter from somebody on campus in which it was stated that nobody on campus was permitted to do business with **No Limits** any more. Even though we did not yet have the store on the campus, we were already the number one supplier to the University. I recognized the letter immediately for what it was – an attack from satan. When he showed me the letter I told him that people make plans, but God has the final say **(Proverbs 16:1 – no weapon formed against us shall prosper)**. The next thing that Gerrit told me was that we had to do a business presentation within the next four weeks – something that is really not my forte. I knew my good friend Deon de Kok would be the right person to help us with it, but he was in Italy at that stage. I would like to interrupt myself briefly and rewind slightly to a time when God told me not to limit Him before any of this had happened. Before God spoke these words to me, I had decided that I was done with No Limits. I saw myself as the pilot of this airplane who had already seen all the limits that were available to be seen. I thought I would take a back seat so that Gerrit and all the other partners could run the business, and I would only share in the profits. I had decided that I would like to become more involved in the property business. During that time, Stephan Pretorius, also a prominent businessman from Potchefstroom and a man of God came to me and said that he saw No Limits as a large airplane that was only taking off, and that we should know that it was going to reach a very high altitude. There would be strong winds, but as long as we kept our eyes on Jesus everything would be all right. (Stephan did not know that I saw myself as the pilot of the plane, planning to let everything go). Stephan shared this with me on a Sunday, and by the very next Wednesday, one of my brothers called *to say that he had a dream about the business – that it was like a balloon that was just expanding. He woke up and immediately realized that a balloon that got too large would inevitably burst. He decided that he would not tell me about the "bad news" part of the dream. The following night, he dreamt about the business again, but then he realized that it was a silicone balloon that could not burst, but that it was too large for me to handle on my own – I had to gather other people to help me hold on to the balloon, and one of the people whose name came up to help was my friend Deon, who was an engineer working in the corporate sector.*

I approached him and told him what we were doing and what our dream was. The seed started growing in his heart, and he felt that he wanted to be a part of the plan. It was during this time that we were asked to tender at the University of Johannesburg and Deon is very good at putting together these kinds of presentations. At the time, Deon was in Italy with the international company that he was working for. They decided, however, to travel to South Africa for some reason at exactly the same time we were due to do the presentation. God sent Deon to us, paid for by another company, to come and help us with our presentation. On the evening before the presentation we worked through the night to get everything finished, and while we were working, the Lord said to me, "Bernard, you keep on saying that this is My business. I want you to tell that to the people at the meeting tomorrow, during the presentation." I immediately said to the Lord: "Lord it doesn't work like that here on earth – people don't say things like that in the corporate world." I asked the other people who were involved what they thought, and their reaction was that there was no way I could (or should) do it. They went so far as to say that if I insisted on doing it they would not even show up at the meeting. I said to the Lord quietly: "Lord, if this feeling is still here tomorrow, then I'll say it, but I really hope I heard wrong, and that this is just something I made up." The following morning, however, the feeling was stronger than ever and I decided to go ahead and do it without telling any of my partners. We didn't have a good time slot for our presentation – among the ten companies doing presentations, we were eighth or ninth. It was already three o'clock in the afternoon, the panel members were tired, they were not in the mood to listen to people any longer or look at more presentations, because every presenter tried to outdo the others and tell a better story. Gerrit presented the introduction and I shared our dream with the panel. Their facial expressions weren't very positive – you could see that there was very little life left in that room. I began by saying: "Ladies and gentlemen, I would like to start this presentation by saying that all the honor and the glory belongs to God, because this business came into existence through Him and therefore, the purpose of this business is to expand God's Kingdom and give Him glory." The moment I had said that, it suddenly felt as if there was a new brightness in the room. Everybody's eyes lit up, and suddenly there was joy in the room - I could feel it in the air. The following morning the fax came through to say that nobody could do business with us any longer. Those who had written that letter didn't even know that we were going to pitch for the store. The University is a large organization, and the one department does not know what the others are doing. The commercial offices dealt with the tender process and the procurement office had sent out the letter. They immediately withdrew the letter, and apologized for it, claiming that it had been sent out by mistake, and that we were back in business again. The tender process took eighteen months, and through the grace of God and His favor, we received the tender and an exclusive five-year contract on the campus of the University of Johannesburg, because this was part of God's plan for No Limits. We praise the Lord for this grace. We received the tender in the face of competition from Adidas, Nike and Canterbury, because Proverbs 16:1 says that man proposes, but God disposes.

When we receive the revelation of the capacity and strength of the seed of faith that is there for each of us, and we begin to implement it, nothing will be impossible.

Bernard's faith determined his actions. Even in the harsh world of business his faith determined his action: which was to honor the name of God during a presentation – something that was not normally even considered. God honored Bernard for that.

I have supported people in crisis situations that appeared absolutely impossible at first – a terminal disease, a financial crisis, or a child who causes stress to the parents. At times, people would be so overwhelmed by the impossibility of the situation, they would say, "My faith is not strong enough for this". However, when we receive the revelation of the capacity and strength of the seed of faith that is there for each of us, and we begin to implement it, nothing will be impossible.

In Mark 9, we read about the man whose child was tormented by a mute spirit. When Jesus arrived on the scene, the man explained the situation to Him, and Jesus responded by saying something remarkable:

"And often he has thrown him both into the fire and into the water to destroy him. But if You can do anything, have compassion on us and help us." Jesus said to him, "If you can believe, all things are possible to him who believes" (Mark 9:22, 23; NKJV)

Everything is possible when you believe, because the faith that we received is not an inferior faith - it is a faith with the same value and ability as the faith Jesus, the apostles and all the heroes of faith who went before us had. The faith that we received is a faith that God wants to use to make His Kingdom a tangible reality for the world. Whatever your personal situation, you carry the faith of Jesus in you, you have the same power that Peter and Paul had within you – it is simply waiting to be activated.

Faith like a mustard seed enables you to command the mountain, or impossibility, to move – and it will obey.

Faith like a mustard seed enables you to command the mountain, or impossibility, to move– and it will obey. The Kingdom of God may be like a seed, but it is strong enough to outgrow, outmaneuver, and overwhelm any worldly system.

5
ACTIVATE YOUR FAITH

SO FAR WE'VE ALREADY DISCUSSED *'What is faith?'*, *'God's gift of grace'* and *'Why faith?'* We've also seen that when you have faith like a mustard seed, and you command the mountain to move, it must move. However, the mountain can only move when you begin to do things differently.

Every single day, we are flooded with information – most of which is negative. It's almost like drinking small doses of poison on a regular basis. It might not affect you immediately, but eventually, it will poison your entire system. Just think of everything you have to deal with on a daily basis. You may find yourself exhausted because of long distance traveling to work every day and being exposed to an endless stream of e-mails, phone calls, text messages, noise, traffic, politics, radio, television, news reports, the neighbors' barking dog, bills, responsibilities, deadlines, the seemingly endless list of things that need to be repaired around the house, whining children, and maybe even the pain of a broken relationship.

What we see and hear, whether good or bad, shapes our world. We become victims of these circumstances. We even feel overwhelmed by other people's problems and the injustices of the world and this is all we seem to talk about. How on earth can we possibly escape from this madness?

Have you ever come home late at night? It's pitch black inside the house, so you fumble around looking for the light switch. When you try turn on the light nothing happens – the light bulb must have blown out. I don't know what your reaction is, but I tend to hit the switch a couple of times just to make sure that it's not working. Usually, if there are people with you, they will do the same – they all try the switch just to make sure the light is really not working. This is exactly how we approach life – we keep on doing the same thing over and over, expecting different results!

This raises the question: "So what should I do differently to get a different result?"

> **Whatever God does in your life, He does on the basis of faith.**

Whatever God does in your life, He does on the basis of faith. I have heard faith being compared to the mainspring of a watch. It is indispensable. It is the mechanism that kicks you into action. Everyone has faith – even an atheist has faith. The only difference is what you are using your faith for and how much faith you have. Consider this chapter a faith-building session. We are going to look at a few principles, and I guarantee they will change your life. You will never be the same again, because these truths are dynamic and revolutionary.

Have you ever said, "I wish I could have more faith?" In Romans 10:17 we read about how you can get more faith:

> *So then faith comes by hearing, and hearing by the word of God.* (NKJV)

According to this scripture, we get more faith by listening to the Word of God. As you read the Bible, you'll learn more and more about how faith can bring about a positive change in your life and your faith will grow.

In Proverbs 4 we read:

> **Hear, my son, and receive my sayings, and the years of your life will be many.** (Proverbs 4:10 NKJV)

It's difficult to describe how important it is for you to "hear" spiritually. Your ears are one of the two natural pathways to your spirit – your eyes being the other. When it comes to God's promises, you cannot receive what you haven't heard. When you read Revelation chapters 2 and 3, you will see that Jesus is serious about us hearing His words. In these two chapters, this is emphasized seven times. When you read Revelation 2 verse 7, 11, 17 and 29 as well as Revelation 3 verse 6, 13 and 22, you'll notice that John repeatedly wrote: "He who has an ear, let him hear what the Spirit says to the churches." I do not doubt for one moment that the Lord is serious about us HEARING what He is saying to us.

The act of hearing

To hear something is relatively simple – it is nothing more than receiving impulses through your ear canal. "Hearing" in Biblical terms, however, involves far more than simply picking up sounds. Biblical hearing requires attentiveness and obedience. Proverbs directly links hearing with receiving.

> **Hear, my son, and receive my sayings, and the years of your life will be many.** (Proverbs 4:10, NKJV)

It is clear from this verse that there is a promise of a long and full life for those who can hear and apply God's words. "Receive" is another way of saying, "obey". If you are not committed to being obedient to the Word of God, you have not really received it. In James 1:22 we read:

> *But be doers of the word, and not hearers only, deceiving yourselves...*

The verse in Proverbs shows us that the eventual result of 'hearing' is the gift of a long life. Hearing results in receiving – there is always a harvest! This is a spiritual process that cannot be stopped or changed. Hear! Receive! Harvest!

Proverbs 8:34 gives us another view on this truth:

> *Blessed is the man who listens to me, Watching daily at my gates, Waiting at the posts of my doors.*
> (Proverbs 8:34, NKJV)

Hearing results in receiving – there is always a harvest! This is a spiritual process that cannot be stopped or changed. Hear! Receive! Harvest!

Blessing is always the result of hearing. To be blessed means to be "empowered for prosperity". True biblical prosperity involves so much more than just money. It involves abundance, peace and an increase in every area of our lives. It doesn't mean escaping from our problems, but rather that we know that our salvation and blessing are on the way. Prosperity gives you the strength to be in control of your circumstances rather than being controlled *by* your circumstances. You gain that sort of strength by hearing God's Word. In other words, whatever you choose to listen to will determine whether or not you are capable of handling the difficult situations the enemy brings to you. Let me make it practical. When you are seriously ill, satan is quick to whisper in your ear, "You're not going to get well. You're going to die." When you regularly hear the Word of healing, however, it empowers you to take charge of the situation and to drive both satan and the symptoms of disease from your life.

"See to it that your Bible remains open, read it, hear it, reflect on it and live every day in the light of His promises."

As I write about this truth, my mind goes back to 2009 when I was diagnosed with the Guillain Barré Syndrome – a viral disease that systematically attacked my whole body. During this time I experienced a great deal of trauma and confusion. Medical specialists were standing next to my bed, arguing about what was wrong with me – you can imagine how I felt, realizing that not even the medical experts understood what was wrong with me. During this time, I went through a death experience where I was clinically dead for 25 minutes, I was assaulted by demons and I was also told that I would never preach again. Never preach again? Preaching is my life! I read through my book, *A Silent Adventure*, which I wrote shortly after this experience, and my eye was drawn to a specific sentence I wrote:

See to it that your Bible remains open, read it, hear it, reflect on it and live every day in the light of His promises.

This literally became my lifeline and salvation. In that time, my vocal chords were paralyzed so I could not speak – all I could do was listen to God's Word. I listened to men and women of God who preached His Word, I listened and I listened and I listened! Have you seen what happens to a sponge if you submerge it in water? It becomes heavy with the water it has absorbed. This is what happened to me as I listened to God's Word. I became like a sponge – absorbing the truth from the Word of God. Even though the odds were never in my favor, and the medical reports said that it was impossible for me to be healed – I chose to keep the Word of God close to me and believe in His Word and His plans for me. His Word reminded me that I was the apple of His eye, that He had good plans in store for me – plans to prosper and not to harm me. God's Word in me enabled me to filter what people were saying around me. The grip that the disease had on me slowly but surely began to relax and I knew that it was because I kept the right words and truth close to me.

You and I cannot allow the news, media or the negative reports about the world to become our focus. Not only is it essential that we hear the Word when facing problems, but it is important that we hear it thoroughly and effectively. How we receive the Word of God can make an enormous difference to what we can and will see. This is precisely what Jesus was saying in Mark 4:24 just after he had told the parable of the sower:

Then He said to them, "Take heed what you hear. With the same measure you use, it will be measured to you; and to you who hear, more will be given. (Mark 4:24, NKJV)

In the New Living Translation this verse is written as follows:

Then he added, "Pay close attention to what you hear. The closer you listen, the more under-

standing you will be given—and you will receive even more. (Mark 4:24, NLT)

From these two translations, it's very clear that we should be careful about who we listen to. Make sure that you listen to the right things and hear the right words because both faith and fear come from what we hear. There may be people in our lives who tell us daily how bad things are - just like Job's friends and wife. If I think back, I realize that there were times when negative words took root in my heart – when I allowed these negative words to hold me back from the truth already in my heart, or what I believed the Lord had told me.

Let's read Romans 10:17 again:

So then faith comes by hearing, and hearing by the word of God. (Romans 10:17, NKJV)

Our problem – Thoughts from the past → Unbelief

In the past, I've often told myself, "Willem, your problem is that your thinking is based on past events rather than the future. You need to think differently." Unbelief looks back to the past and says, "Look, this can't be done. "Faith, however, looks at the future and says, "This can be done, and according to the promises of God, it WILL be done!" Faith demotes the failures of the past and gives you the courage to go and face every situation as if the victory has already been achieved.

Faith, however, looks at the future and says, "This can be done, and according to the promises of God, it WILL be done!"

Faith and fear cannot co-exist. There is no place for stress or fear in faith. When watching a big sports game, you may have seen how the two captains and the referee stand in the middle of the pitch and toss a coin into the air before the game begins. The captain of the home team is usually allowed to toss the coin, and the visiting captain can then call "heads" or "tails". The captain that wins the toss can then make certain decisions about the coming game. It has never happened that the referee announced that both captains won the toss because heads and tails were on the same side of the coin. This cannot happen – it is impossible because these are two sides of a coin. In the same way, faith and fear are two sides of the coin. It's either fear or faith. Yet there are many Christians who are under the impression that you can have both in your life – in other words, six of one and half a dozen of the other. This is why Christians have little or no impact in society. God created us to effect change, to live in accordance with His promises and His Word. He created us to live BY FAITH. It is only through the FULL Good News (the Gospel) and believing the Word of God in its FULLNESS that we will have a positive impact on this earth and live according to our God-given purpose. In Ephesians 6 we read:

> *For we do not wrestle against flesh and blood, but against principalities, against powers, against the rulers of the darkness of this age against spiritual hosts of wickedness in the heavenly places.* (Ephesians 6:12, NKJV)

In the Phillips translation, this verse reads as follows:

> *For our fight is not against any physical enemy. It is against organizations and powers that are spiritual. We are up against the unseen power*

that controls this dark world and spiritual agents from the very headquarters of evil. (Ephesians 6:12, Phillips translation)

A lady in our church told me about a website she subscribed to. She decided to subscribe because that particular website would send out all sorts of news reports and interesting bits of information every day. Initially she did not notice, but most of the news items that were sent to her dealt with murder, missing persons and other crimes. Whenever she heard a dog barking, she would be completely gripped by fear – she would lie awake at night and allow fear to build up in her heart. After a few weeks of feeling like this she realized that something was wrong. It's not that she wanted to ignore the facts or avoid reality, but the fact that she had constantly been hearing negative news had begun to cultivate an unhealthy fear in her own mind, which directly impacted her behavior. She immediately decided to cancel her subscription and three days later all her fears had gone. This proves, yet again, that fear and faith cannot co-exist.

Both fear and faith come through words – *rhema* word

It might sound strange to say this, but if you can fear, you can also have faith. Both faith and fear work on the same principle. Fear comes to you through what you hear. In Romans 10:8 we read:

But what does it say? "The word is near you, in your mouth and in your heart" (that is, the word of faith which we preach) (Romans 10:8, NKJV)

In Matthew 9, it is very interesting to note Jesus' reaction when they brought a paralyzed man to Him. We read:

Then behold, they brought to Him a paralytic lying on a bed. When Jesus saw their faith, He said to the paralytic, "Son, be of good cheer; your sins are forgiven you. (Matthew 9:2, NKJV)

Jesus is actually saying, "Don't worry. You are not a burden to me." You and I sometimes feel like we're a burden to Him, and we forget that we're actually the apple of His eye. THE FIRST THING THAT JESUS DOES IS TO ADDRESS THIS MAN'S FEARS AND TO REASSURE HIM!

Fear is a universal problem. If you simply suppress the fears and worries in your heart, they are likely to turn into depression. Depression is almost always a result of suppressed anger or fear. Proverbs 12 says:

Anxiety in the heart of man causes depression, But a good word makes it glad. (Proverbs 12:25, NKJV)

This is what Jesus did with the paralyzed man. He began by giving him an encouraging word. What are we supposed to do with our fears and anxieties? We give them to Jesus Christ. In 1 Peter 5:7 we read:

... casting all your care upon Him, for He cares for you. (1 Peter 5:7, NKJV)

I would like you to read this verse again, and then to circle the word *all*. It does not say, "cast some" or "only a few" of your worries – it says **ALL**. I looked up the word, "all" in the dictionary, and astonishingly, it meant just that. All. *Everything.* This verse tells us we should cast everything onto Him, because Jesus cares for us. The Bible does not say, "Perfect love drives out all fear" for nothing.

I would like to come back to Romans 10:8 that says:

But what does it say? "The word is near you, in your mouth and in your heart" (that is, the word of faith which we preach)."

This is how it works:

Faith comes by **hearing**.

Hearing comes by the **Word**.

Faith really comes by the word that I allow NEAR me – in my mouth and in my heart. I therefore allow certain words close to me – these are the words I speak (in my mouth) and they remain in my heart and yield a harvest. If I can regulate and filter the WORD that comes close to me, I can also regulate the type of harvest I will receive. This is why it is so important for the heart to be full of the Word. Let's take some time to talk about the state of your heart. Look at the following Scripture in Mark 4 and see what Jesus had to say to His disciples:

> **Faith really comes by the word that I allow NEAR me – in my mouth and in my heart.**

And He said to them, "Do you not understand this parable? How then will you understand all the parables? The sower sows the word. And these are the ones by the wayside where the word is sown. When they hear, Satan comes immediately and takes away the word that was sown in their hearts. These likewise are the ones sown on stony ground who, when they hear the word, immediately receive it with gladness; and they have no root in themselves, and so endure only for a time. Afterward, when tribulation or persecution arises for the word's sake, immediately they stumble. Now these are the ones sown among thorns; they are the ones who hear the word, and the cares of this world, the deceitfulness of riches, and the desires for other things entering in choke the word, and it becomes unfruitful. But these are the ones sown on good ground, those who hear the word, accept it, and bear fruit: some thirtyfold, some sixty, and some a hundred. (Mark 4:13-20, NKJV)

You see, we hear the Word but then we respond like the people did in this passage:

- As soon as they hear the Word, satan steals the Word through unbelief.
- Others have hardened hearts and they hear the Word but there is no fertile ground.
- Most people, however, are like those who hear the Word, but it falls among the WEEDS.

He describes weeds as the cares of life, the deceitfulness of riches, and the greed for things that are not ours! The process works like this:

- Our worries strangle the Word, and nullify its power.
- Our quest for wealth and fame further nullifies the effect of the Seed that has already been made powerless by our cares and worries, so that it does not bear fruit.

- Lastly, the seed that has not yet been choked out by the first two weeds will be strangled by the temptations and seductions of life. These temptations want to come and dwell in our hearts. Unlike the other two weeds, we are seduced by these temptations into a prison of unhealthy habits, such as eating, gossiping, pornography, alcohol abuse or any other habit-forming substance.

Let's have a look at what the Bible has to say about our hearts. In Proverbs 4:23 we read the following:

> **Keep your heart with all diligence, for out of it spring the issues of life.** (Proverbs 4:23, NKJV)

If Proverbs tells us that our heart determines everything that happens in our life, it is essential to pause and reflect on the heart for a moment.

The Heart

Your heart is your body's pacemaker. It determines whether you are capable of doing things or not. It holds your emotions, will and life. It helps to form your thoughts. Your heart is the central power station of your life. There are nine descriptive words that can be used for the heart, namely (1) Organ that sustains blood circulation in the body; (2) Bosom; (3) Health condition; (4) Mind; (5) Courage; (6) Pith or core; (7) Essence; (8) Inner being and (9) Beloved.

Proverbs 4:23 simply re-enforces what we read in Romans 10: 8 – **Near to you is the word in your mouth and in your heart.** That which is planted in our hearts as a result of the words we speak, has a powerful effect on what is happening in our lives. In Proverbs 27 we read:

As in water face reflects *face, So a man's heart* reveals *the man.* (Proverbs 27:19, NKJV)

Just like in a mirror, your facial expressions reflect what is really going on in your heart. Over years, I think our facial expressions become marked permanently by whatever is in our hearts. Jesus tells us that our mouths speak from the overflow of our hearts. These words, in turn, come and dwell in our hearts and are expressed on our faces, coming full circle. The WORD of God can be described as spiritual BOTOX. It removes the marks left by our bad life experiences and like an expensive face cream it softens our facial expressions.

In Ecclesiastes 9 we read the following:

This is an evil in all that is done under the sun: that one thing happens to all. Truly the hearts of the sons of men are full of evil; madness is in their hearts while they live, and after that they go to the dead. (Ecclesiastes 9:3b, NKJV)

Once again, Solomon reveals that a person's heart is a breeding ground for evil, the FRUIT of which is FOOLISHNESS. Consequently, this leads to death – not only a physical death, but also the death of dreams, ideals, insights and ultimately relationships. Therefore, whoever protects their heart, also protects Godly ideas, insights, concepts, dreams, ideals and ultimately strategic life-giving relationships.

In Ecclesiastes 11 Solomon says the following:

Therefore remove sorrow from your heart, and put away evil from your flesh, for childhood and youth are vanity. (Ecclesiastes 11:10, NKJV)

Carrying worry and anxiety in your heart will make you physically and spiritually ill. These worries grip your heart and are released into your body like poison. Let's read a few examples in Matthew and Mark where it is clear that problems come from the heart:

Our hearts can, therefore, be a breeding ground for both GOOD and EVIL things.

But I say to you that whoever looks at a woman to lust for her has already committed adultery with her in his heart. (Matthew 5:28, NKJV)

For where your treasure is, there your heart will be also. (Matthew 6:21, NKJV)

Brood of vipers! How can you, being evil, speak good things? For out of the abundance of the heart the mouth speaks. (Matthew 12:34, NKJV)

He answered and said to them, "Well did Isaiah prophesy of you hypocrites, as it is written: This people honors Me with their lips, But their heart is far from Me. (Mark 7:6, NKJV)

For from within, out of the heart of men, proceed evil thoughts, adulteries, fornications, murders... (Mark 7:21, NKJV)

Our hearts can, therefore, be a breeding ground for both GOOD and EVIL things. This is confirmed in Jeremiah 17:

The heart is deceitful above all things, and desperately wicked; Who can know it? (Jeremiah 17:9, NKJV)

So often, people have said to me, "Willem, I only said or wrote what was in my heart" – as if the heart was neutral ground. Jeremiah had a vastly different opinion and described the heart as deceitful. I can hear you protesting, "Surely it's a bit harsh to say that? Deceitful is a strong word to use." Just think about it for a moment – if you are listening to things that are UNHOLY and then speaking about them, they will take up residence in your heart. Your heart may well become a deceitful and evil place, but it need not stay that way. In Ezekiel 11 we read:

> **"Lord, please give me a new heart. Help me to keep Your Word and Your plan securely in my new heart. Lord, may I be a hearer and doer of Your Word, bearing much fruit."**

Then I will give them one heart, and I will put a new spirit within them and take the stony heart out of their flesh, and give them a heart of flesh. (Ezekiel 11:19, NKJV)

This makes me want to shout, "Hallelujah! Praise the Lord!" What a promise. As you're reading this, don't you want to pray the following with me? "Lord, please give me a new heart. Help me to keep Your Word and Your plan securely in my new heart. Lord, may I be a hearer and doer of Your Word, bearing much fruit."

The Lord completely changed my heart and called me into ministry with that Scripture. Let me share a story from my own life with you. I used to be really interested in politics. Political events and political news have always fascinated me, so much so that when my Grade 8 (Junior High) teacher asked me what I wanted to become, I was serious when I answered, "President of the country!" I have always believed that I could be instrumental in the process of transformation in our country. Unfortunately my political aspirations were fueled by fear and not faith. During school, I actively participated in political debates, and later at University I became a member of a right-wing group, known for their racial hatred and inciting action. At that stage I was a College student, busy with politics full-time. I was involved with the student newspaper, the student radio station, and later on I also served in the student parliament on campus. I served on provincial political structures in our country and was actually a potential candidate for parliament at one point.

Following a recruitment tour I went home to visit my parents. When I arrived, they wanted me to attend a church service with them. I decided to go but had no idea it would be a prophetic service. At the end of the service one of the speakers prophesied over my sister and me. I was so afraid in that moment! What if he began listing all my sins in front of my parents? What he said, however, was that God would remove my heart of stone and replace it with a heart of flesh. He also said God would give me visions of people in hell and that He had called me to lead people to Him. When we got home I called my girlfriend at the time and asked whether she was going to serve the Lord with me. She got the fright of her life and I think she's probably still running now! It was unthinkable for her that I would resign from all my political positions. It wasn't long before I met my wife, Celesté, and the Lord confirmed my calling soon after that.

I think my most significant personal transformation came about when I met Pastor Anthony Constance of Potchefstroom.

He taught me the true meaning of transformation. He had a great influence on me becoming a bridge-builder in our town. The local newspaper published a story on Celesté and me when we arrived in Potchefstroom. This story is clear evidence that the Lord always fulfills his Word, because He had removed my heart of stone and given me a heart of flesh – a heart with a passion for people of all races.

Pastoor Willem Nel en sy vrou, Celesté.

Herald kuier by pastoor Willem Nel

Vir 'n jong pastorie-egpaar is die rustigheid van Potchefstroom net die regte medisyne na nege en 'n half jaar in Johannesburg. "Hier", sê hulle "kan jy nog rustig in die aand vir 'n wandeling gaan."

Die Herald het by pastoor Willem Nel en sy vrou Celesté gaan inloer. Willem is die pastoor van die Potch AGS Studente Kerk. Hulle is reeds twee jaar in Potchefstroom. Hy was ook vir 'n jaar kapelaan in die Weermag gewees.

Willem sê hulle het dié gemeente in 1993 begin en wat die ge-meente uniek maak, is dat dit die eerste Pink-ster Charismatiese ge-meente is wat net stu-dente bedien. Dié ge-meente staan onder voogskap van die AGS Sentraal Gemeente.

Die Nel-egpaar glo hulle is spesifiek Pot-chefstroom toe geroep om brûe tussen mense en kerkgroepe te bou.

Hulle is veral daarop toegespits om onreg-verdigheid van die ver-lede aan te spreek.

Willem en Celesté is oud-Raukies en wat hulle veral van die studente in Potchef-stroom opgeval het was

dat hierdie studente nog "mens-mense" is. Willem en Celesté het mekaar op RAU by In-tervarsity ontmoet en hulle is na hulle oplei-ding getroud.

Willem is ook betrok-ke by die Nasionale Studentebediening en hou hom veral besig met rekenaars. Celesté sê haar man hou van tegnologie wat die lewe vergemaklik.

Celesté is nie net ak-tief betrokke by die studente nie, maar sy is ook betrokke by die op-leiding van kinderbe-diening. Verder hou sy haarself besig met naaldwerk.

The Herald newspaper in conversation with Pastor Willem Nel:

For a young couple in the ministry, the tranquility of Potchefstroom is just what the doctor ordered after nine and a half years in Johannesburg. "You can still go for a quiet walk in the evenings here," they said.

The Herald visited Pastor Willem Nel and his wife Celesté. Willem is the pastor of the Potchefstroom Apostolic Faith Mission Student Church. They have been in Potchefstroom now for almost two years. He was also a chaplain in the Defense Force for a year.

Willem says that they started this congregation in 1993 and what makes it unique is that it is the first Pentecostal Charismatic church that ministers exclusively to students. This congregation is under the patronage of the AFS Central Congregation.

The Nels believe they have specifically been called to Potchefstroom to help build bridges between people and church groups. They also focus specifically on addressing the wrongs of the past.

Willem and Celesté are both alumni of the former Rand Afrikaans University and what really struck them about the Potchefstroom students is that they are genuine "peoples-people." Willem and Celesté met each other at RAU during the Inter-universities sports day and got married after completing their studies.

Willem is also involved in the National Students' Ministry and has a special interest in computers. Celesté says that her husband likes technology that simplifies one's life.

Celesté is not only actively involved with the students, but is also involved in training people for children's ministry. She also likes sewing.

The Word promises that you will SEE GOD as a result of having a new heart. We read about this in Matthew 5:

> **Blessed are the pure in heart, for they shall see God.** (Matthew 5:8, NKJV)

FAITH is the result of a heart turned toward God and His WORD. In Mark 11 Jesus shows us what can happen when we really demonstrate faith:

> **For assuredly, I say to you, whoever says to this mountain, 'Be removed and be cast into the sea,' and does not doubt in his heart, but believes that those things he says will be done, he will have whatever he says.** (Mark 11:23, NKJV)

Love is the result of us giving our WHOLE HEARTS to God.

> **And you shall love the LORD your God with all your heart, with all your soul, with all your mind, and with all your strength.' This is the first commandment.** (Mark 12:30, NKJV)

The Lord is intensely interested in the sincerity of our hearts. He is not so much interested in what we can give Him or do for Him. We see this in Mark 12:33:

> **And to love Him with all the heart, with all the understanding, with all the soul, and with all the strength, and to love one's neighbor as oneself, is more than all the whole burnt offerings and sacrifices.** (Mark 12:33, NKJV)

- YOUR HEART is the treasure chest of your life.
- Your life's purpose flows from YOUR HEART.
- YOUR HEART is the source of your emotions, will and thoughts – in other words, YOUR SOUL.
- God desires to have YOUR HEART.
- YOUR HEART is filled with whatever you see.

God desires to come and live in your heart. We read this in Ephesians 3:17, and I specifically want to quote the Amplified Bible:

> *May Christ through your faith [actually] dwell (settle down, abide, make His permanent home) in your hearts! May you be rooted deep in love and founded securely on love...* (Ephesians 3:17, AMP)

In the first chapter, *'What is Faith?'* I said that faith means taking the initiative. Taking initiative means that you need to activate your faith. Let's have a look at the passage in Mark 5 that deals with the woman with the issue of blood.

This woman had already been suffering for twelve years. She was considered ceremonially unclean by the Jews because her bleeding never stopped. She was not allowed to appear in public or be with people and she, therefore had no social life at all.

One day, however, she heard that Jesus was coming to her town. She told herself, "If I could just touch his robe, I will be healed. She decided to take the initiative and took a very bold step. She not only appeared in public but she pushed her way through the crowd until she was within touching distance of Jesus. When she touched His robe she was healed immediately.

Jesus immediately recognized the touch of faith, and asked,

"Who touched Me?" There was a whole crowd of people around Him and they were all trying to touch Him. This woman had literally forced her way through the crowd to get to Him. The disciples themselves must have touched Jesus, just trying to keep the crowd under control. Peter, surprised by Jesus' question, responded in his usual forthright manner, "What do You mean, 'Who touched You?' Can't You see the crowd of people around You?"

Jesus, however, knew the difference. The woman trembled as she approached Him. "I touched You, Lord." Jesus answered, "Daughter, your faith has made you well."

She took the initiative. She broke the rules of her culture, and moved beyond the restrictions placed on her by society. She activated her faith and pushed through the crowds. She took the initiative and her act of faith healed her. In order to activate your faith, you need to make a conscious decision to begin. You must commit yourself to action.

> **In order to activate your faith, you need to make a conscious decision to begin. You must commit yourself to action.**

Faith is the antidote to procrastination. How does faith help me shift gears and get out of the rut I'm in? How does faith help me move forward, to take that first step that will point me in the direction of my desired destination? How does faith help me overcome indecision so that I don't sit on the fence and change my mind all the time? How can I take initiative? Faith empowers my imagination and enables me to take action!

When you hear the Word of God, the following Godly process takes place:

You allow His Word to come close to you

His Word is a light or a revelation to you

The light brings clarity or understanding (your mind understands the revelation)

When you understand you begin to trust

Trust gives you a place to stand

A place to stand gives you a platform

You must decide – will you act or remain passive? Your obedience to the Word that brings light will proceed into action [a deed]. This is a calculated risk that you take, because your trust is in a good and faithful God. Passivity will make you procrastinate and eventually it will make you give up.

In this chapter I have already referred to Romans 10:17 a few times that says,

... *faith* comes *by hearing, and hearing by the word of God.*

I have also mentioned that both faith and fear come to you, and work on the same principle.

When you begin to focus on what you hear or see in the news, you can't help being negative. It is essential to rather concentrate on the good than on the bad. Be careful to tolerate a lot of negative talk from people around you – it will simply get stuck in your head. Rather ask people to keep their negative views to themselves. This does not mean that you ignore the statistics and facts and pretend they do not exist – it just means that these things are not your focus. God's Word is your focus!

How do negative things become a stronghold in my life? Perhaps it is difficult for you to forgive someone, for example. When you say, "I will not forgive you," you are giving those words power. The moment you say those words you are opening a door to satan and consequently allowing these negative things in your life. The only way to get out of this is by saying, "Lord, I am so sorry that I have given myself the right to not forgive. Lord, I choose to forgive others unconditionally, as You have forgiven me." Nobody deserves or can earn God's forgiveness. You need to extend forgiveness to people unconditionally. You also need to forgive specific things so you don't leave a door open for the enemy to sneak in!

6
LIVING IN THE SPIRIT

IT GOES WITHOUT SAYING that we will face many challenges in our lives. Life isn't fair, but God is. He has always been just and fair. I want to begin this chapter by sharing Willem's story (another Willem) with you. He had a radical encounter with Jesus in the midst of hopeless circumstances and went from someone who did not know Jesus at all to someone who serves him wholeheartedly. Here is his story:

My name is Willem, I am 52 years old and single. I am a child of God Almighty who created heaven and earth. Both my parents were alcoholics. My dad was a wife-beater: violence and the most horrific swearing was commonplace in our home, every day. From a young age my dad rejected me and often told me that he didn't want me. In fact, he said he would like to exchange me for a kid from the orphanage. Orphanage! Sometimes I prayed that he would make good on this threat, that he would actually do it. To me, the orphanage sounded like ... Utopia. I just wanted to get away from the violence and havoc and lack of sleep and shame and embarrassment and rejection and humiliation and secrecy and fear and ... and ...

School was hell on earth – each and every day of it. I

wasn't big or strong and I was a sensitive child. What does a child do if he has no idea how to defend himself and lacks the vocabulary to explain how he feels? Psychologically, there may be a whole range of reactions. I escaped into my own make-belief world. I also hardened myself emotionally and I protected myself by erecting walls around me to shield me from everything. These walls kept me prisoner and inhibited me throughout my life.

I started drinking at a really young age and the drinking got worse as I became more desperate and lonely. I hated myself and believed that everyone else hated me too. Of course, drugs also played a role – marijuana was one of the drugs I quite often used. By the age of 40 I was a wreck. My life was a dump and I could see no future whatsoever. After yet another suicide attempt, a friend told me about Buddhism and all the philosophies associated with this belief system. I began reading about Buddhism, but soon I became more interested in the New Age movement. Before long, I became involved in this movement. I finally felt like I was getting answers to life's most profound questions and I began to feel happier. However, this was all an illusion.

When I was 42 I had to move out of my hometown due to circumstances beyond my control. I decided to settle in a small town in the Transkei (one of South Africa's former homelands under Apartheid). This place was very focused on New Age. I wanted to continue with my new life there. On my way there, I had to spend a few days in Durban. At that stage, it had been a year since I had had my last drink and I was quite sure that I had everything under control, especially as far as alcohol was concerned. I then had a beer and smoked a cigarette – one beer and *one cigarette was enough to trigger everything all over again. There and then I gave up all hope of ever being saved. I was busy planning my next suicide attempt when the barman approached me and told me that they needed someone to help them to smuggle dollars into South Africa from Mozambique. If I was willing to help, I could earn R20, 000 (about $2,000). I had no money left and was desperate. It was a case of "do or die." However, the "dollars" turned out to be cocaine, and the Mozambican police caught me red-handed. Today I know that I wasn't used as a drug mule, but as bait – the person who drew the attention of the police away, so that the real mules could pass through unseen, as they had done so many times.*

I thought that this was the end – the end that came so differently from how I had planned it. I had seen documentaries on life in South African prisons, showing all the horrible things that happen in prisons to people of all ages. These images kept haunting me while I spent two days in police custody. I was then sent to a maximum-security prison where I spent 9 years and 10 months of my life.

I was robbed on my very first day in prison, but apart from that, there were very few violent incidences. I'm forever grateful to the Lord for that. Life in a third-world prison is no picnic, and not something I would wish on my worst enemy. It was sheer hell. I thank God that I have a sister, Anita, who stood by me faithfully for the almost 10 years that I was in prison. With her help I could survive in a fairly civilized manner. Many of Anita's friends and people in her Bible study group also supported me faithfully during my term in prison.

We were given very little food in prison, and what we were given was basically inedible. Apart from constant hunger, sickness was rampant. If you became ill and did not have money on you, you were simply left to suffer and die. The government provided medicine, but the corrupt officials stole everything and sold it. There were no toothbrushes, toothpaste, soap or any other toiletries. Not even a bowl for food. No uniform or other clothes were given to us. No beds or bedding. We had to sleep on the cold cement floor and believe me it could get cold – especially in winter and even more so when it rained. I thank God for Anita who provided money and other things – thanks to her, I lived in relative comfort compared to most of the inmates. One of the inmates gave me a thin mattress and later on I inherited an iron bed when another inmate had served his term and was discharged.

I remember many charitable gestures, and I have much to be grateful for. The Lord healed me of any trace of racism during those hard years. However, I became a prisoner of my own thoughts. I had a great deal of time to think – and I thought about anything and everything. Who was I? What did I want? Why was I here at this point in my life? I must add that liquor, drugs and cigarettes were freely available in that prison. I didn't have any money, but a few times each year I made plans for a good drinking session. The last of these took place on New Year's Eve, 2007, and since then I've been free of even a desire to drink. The Heavenly Father delivered me from this need!

Mozambique is a Portuguese-speaking country and there were no English Bibles, and of course, no Afrikaans ones either. I felt a great need to read the Bible. Initially I could resist this urge, because in my New Age belief system, there was no place for God. He didn't exist. Besides, I could not imagine that the God of my youth would want me, and to be honest, I didn't want that God, either. He's our Dad, after all, and my experiences of father figures did not exactly inspire much confidence in a relationship with a Father. At the same time however, I found myself doubting my New Age beliefs. I certainly wasn't where the spirit mediums and fortunetellers or my "angel charts" and crystals told me I would be.

After a few weeks of a constant nagging desire to lay my hands and eyes on a Bible, I asked my sister to send me one. Telephones were prohibited, but thanks to corruption anything could be arranged, as long as you had money. I borrowed someone's phone and quickly called Anita. I had to wait a few weeks for the Afrikaans Bible, but I eventually got it. I read it from cover to cover. Still a little skeptical, I sensed something stirring inside of me. My experience is difficult to explain but I gave my life to Jesus, unconditionally.

By 2008 my ability to understand Portuguese was such that I could attend the Manna Church – a charismatic evangelical church. It was then that the devil really began to play tricks on me. I think he realized that I was serious, I really belonged to God and I had forsaken EVERYTHING that he had used to keep me in chains my whole life up to that point. I was also baptized that year, in an inflatable swimming pool.

This was no easy path, and I'm not talking about prison here. That was difficult enough, and I don't ever want to relive a single day there, but I'm strangely grateful for the experience. It turned out to be a great blessing. I'm so thankful that the Father was able to use those horrific circumstances to make me into a new person, the person I am today. It may have been the only way He could get my attention, and I am grateful that He instilled in me the desire to seek HIM.

Today I'm free from any craving for alcohol or cigarettes. From time to time I am still attacked by depression, but I am able to recognize it now, and I know where it comes from. I fight it with all my spiritual armor and weapons, and before long it leaves me. These days, depression does not last for longer than a day, and it certainly doesn't hit me as severely as it used to when it felt like I was completely cloaked and smothered in darkness for weeks on end.

I praise the Father, and I thank Him every day for His grace and love that carried me through these dark times – and still carry me. I thank Him for all the wonderful people He sent along the way. My Father promised me that He would restore me and heal me, and that He would give back to me all that the locusts devoured – everything that the enemy took from me. This is already under way. His Word never comes back empty. What an amazing God!

Wow, what a testimony! When Willem shared his story in church recently, he said, "It is not what you have done, it is what you have overcome." In this chapter, I want to take this thought further and help answer some profound questions that you may have – in particular, the questions you ask when things are not going well. I not only want to answer these questions, but also show you how to live by faith in a practical, day-to-day manner.

How do you live by faith PRACTICALLY?

In James 1:2 we read:

> *My brethren, count it all joy when you fall into various trials ...* (James 1:2, NKJV)

When you read different translations of the Bible, you will see that the word trials used here is sometimes translated as *temptations* or *difficulties*. The statement that James makes in this verse is by no means a promise of God's punishment. Rather, he is simply saying that trials are a fact of life! In his letter, James, the brother of Jesus, is telling us to be on the lookout for these things. Trials or difficulties happen to good and bad people. Temptations don't stop to ask who you are. Difficulty finds each and every one of us at some point. It's not something we deserve or don't deserve – but one thing we can be sure of, is that it WILL cross your path at some point in your life. James says that when problems come your way, you should use them as an opportunity to practice joy. I always say that when you stand before a problem, you should regard it as a compliment from heaven, because the Lord knew that He could impact the circumstances through your life and change the outcome through His glory and might in you.

Let me return to James for a moment. James says that temptations, difficulties, trials, problems, and bad things should be used as opportunities for experiencing JOY. "Uh ... sorry if I sound a bit harsh here, James, but have you completely lost your mind? How on earth can you find joy when bad things happen to you or when trials and tribulations overwhelm you?" I'm sure you have asked many similar questions. Only masochists enjoy pain and discomfort – normal people prefer things to go well. However, James says here that these trials are an OPPORTUNITY for JOY. Nehemiah stood before the people who were crying over the words of the law they had heard. In their time of great difficulty and need, Nehemiah tells them:

Do not sorrow, for the joy of the Lord is your strength. (Nehemiah 8:10, NKJV)

When speaking to the Philippians, Paul supports this statement by saying:

Rejoice in the Lord always. Again I will say, rejoice! (Philippians 4:4, NKJV)

In the Living Bible, this verse is translated as follows:

Always be full of joy in the Lord; I say it again, rejoice! (Philippians 4:4, LB)

I have a friend who understands the importance of this principle in my life. Some time ago he bought me a cover for my mobile phone, with the following words imprinted on it, "The Joy of the Lord is my strength." The reason this is so important to me is because it is in my nature to feel negative, or even to become depressed when I face uncomfortable or difficult situations. Everything in me calls to Jesus the Savior, as I really don't want to endure the trial – I would honestly prefer to avoid it completely. It almost feels as if I'm a student, who on the night before a big exam wonders "Isn't there anybody who'll stand in for me and do this in my place?" My three Bible coaches - James, the apostle Paul and the prophet Nehemiah are all very clear in their advice for dealing with this situation – REJOICE when you face difficulties.

Francois du Toit wrote the following:

Jesus is the origin and the fulfillment of our faith. He is the

*source and its confirmation at the same time (Heb.12:2).
Man's salvation is not at risk; it is not being weighed to
check its worth! It is a done deal! God isn't still in a process
of making a decision, the outcome of which we have yet to
be informed! In Jesus God has already said YES to you!*

After reading these words, I understood that we need the joy of
the Lord. I realized that His joy is like a shield in tough times, and
His joy is part of the Kingdom, as we read in Romans 14:17-18:

*... for the kingdom of God is not eating and
drinking, but righteousness and peace and joy in
the Holy Spirit. For he who serves Christ in these
things is acceptable to God and approved by men.*
(Romans 14:17-18, NKJV)

Joy does not come from an external source: it comes from within
us. God has made us more than conquerors. His plan is for us
to experience His fullness. He wants us to experience victory,
not defeat. He has not planned bad things for us but wants us
to experience REAL LIFE. This God-given truth is why Psalm
18 means so much to me. Allow Him to reveal His power to you,
regardless of the circumstances you may find yourself in. As you
read Psalm 18, may you also experience the revelation of God's
greatness. I pray that the Holy Spirit will encourage you through
His Word and that the JOY of the Lord will reign over your
thoughts as you read the following extracts from this Psalm:

*The Lord is my rock and my fortress and my
deliverer; My God, my strength, in whom I will
trust; My shield and the horn of my salvation, my
stronghold.*

The Lord is a safe place, a solid rock where we can find refuge. These are His words, and He fulfills His words.

I will call upon the Lord, who is worthy to be praised; so shall I be saved from my enemies.

I will persist and praise the Lord!

The pangs of death surrounded me, and the floods of ungodliness made me afraid. The sorrows of Sheol surrounded me; the snares of death confronted me. In my distress I called upon the Lord, and cried out to my God; He heard my voice from His temple, and my cry came before Him, even to His ears.

Say these words with me: Lord, even if the enemy and his evil forces surround me, I am safe with You. Evil has no authority over me or over my family. Lord, You protect me completely. I will no longer fear. I speak YOUR NAME over myself and over my circumstances. Your Word says in Ephesians 1 that Your Name is higher than everything else – every power, every principality, every authority and every name, not only in this world, but also the world to come. Now prayerfully read the following and pray it over your life and your circumstances:

I will call upon the Lord, who is worthy to be praised; so shall I be saved from my enemies. The pangs of death surrounded me, and the floods of ungodliness made me afraid.

The sorrows of Sheol surrounded me; the snares of death confronted me. In my distress I called upon the Lord, and cried out to my God; He heard my voice from His temple, and my cry came before Him, even to His ears. Then the earth shook and trembled; the foundations of the hills also quaked and were shaken, because He was angry. Smoke went up from His nostrils, and devouring fire from His mouth; coals were kindled by it. He bowed the heavens also, and came down with darkness under His feet.

And He rode upon a cherub, and flew; He flew upon the wings of the wind. He made darkness His secret place; His canopy around Him was dark waters and thick clouds of the skies. From the brightness before Him, His thick clouds passed with hailstones and coals of fire. The Lord thundered from heaven, and the Most High uttered His voice, hailstones and coals of fire. He sent out His arrows and scattered the foe, lightnings in abundance, and He vanquished them. Then the channels of the sea were seen, the foundations of the world were uncovered At Your rebuke, O Lord, at the blast of the breath of Your nostrils.

He sent from above, He took me; He drew me out of many waters. He delivered me from my strong enemy, from those who hated me, for they were too strong for me. They confronted me in the day of my calamity, but the Lord was my support. He also brought me out into a broad place; He delivered me because He delighted in me. The Lord rewarded me according to my righteousness; according to the cleanness of my hands He has recompensed me. For I have kept the ways of the

Lord, and have not wickedly departed from my God. For all His judgments were before me, and I did not put away His statutes from me. I was also blameless before Him, and I kept myself from my iniquity. Therefore the Lord has recompensed me according to my righteousness, according to the cleanness of my hands in His sight.

With the merciful You will show Yourself merciful; with a blameless man You will show Yourself blameless; with the pure You will show Yourself pure; and with the devious You will show Yourself shrewd. For You will save the humble people, but will bring down haughty looks. For You will light my lamp; The Lord my God will enlighten my darkness. For by You I can run against a troop, by my God I can leap over a wall. *As for God, His way is perfect; the word of the Lord is proven; He is a shield to all who trust in Him. For who is God, except the Lord? And who is a rock, except our God?* (Psalm 18:3-31, NKJV)

> **God does not save us out of pity; instead, He redeems His image and likeness in us.**

God does not save us out of pity; instead, He redeems His image and likeness in us. The Greek word for "count it all joy" (James 1:2, NKJV) is *"hegeomai"* which is the intensive form of the word *"ago"* which means to guide, like a shepherd guides his sheep. In the Biblical context, a shepherd referred to a leader or someone with authority. He needed to protect his sheep against the elements, against thieves and wild animals. The word *"hegeomai"* therefore means to have an official appointment;

to be charged with official authority. It also means to reign over something. We should therefore allow joy to officially take charge of our circumstances! Joy is not giving a half-hearted smile while you're actually busy licking your wounds and feeling sorry for yourself. No! Joy is the dominant force that reigns in your spirit, while you may be feeling the opposite. The most sensible decision you could ever make in the midst of difficult circumstances is always one that yields joy. Always remember that joy is not something you DO, but rather the fruit of what you KNOW.

Joy understands that you are one with your Creator. Joy is the voice of faith. Joy responds to what faith knows. The moment joy becomes the official authority in your life you will find that feelings of anxiety, self-pity, seeking sympathy, and complaining about insignificant problems or comparing your problems with others will become meaningless. If joy does not assume authority over your circumstances, you will certainly respond in this manner. These kinds of responses cause you to remain bound by insecurities and weakness. In the New Testament, the Greek word used to describe joy is *"karah"*. This word means favor, joy and health, to move ahead. God's plan for us is never one that takes us backwards. His plan is for us to be surrounded with His joy.

I've already mentioned that trials and difficulties are part of life. How can you possibly feel glad if it seems like everything in your life is falling apart? The answer is simple, and you may have heard it several times before. I can rejoice in difficult circumstances if I shift my focus away from myself and focus completely on Him. He is the AUTHOR and the PERFECTER of my faith. How do I keep my focus on Him alone? By praising Him for WHO He is. In Psalm 121 David asks:

I lift up my eyes to the hills—Where does my help come from?

He provides the answer himself:

My help comes from the Lord, Who made heaven and earth. He who keeps you will not slumber. Behold, He who keeps Israel shall neither slumber nor sleep.

Isaiah also asks the question – WHO formed the earth, and WHO measured the waters? The answer - God - the Creator of all.

How do I focus on Him? When I praise the Lord, my focus shifts directly to HIM. Praise and worship changes everything because it changes your perspective of the problem. When you worship God, your own needs become insignificant and His power and presence overwhelms you. Sometimes we are so consumed by needs and problems that we fail to see God at all. Don't allow your relationship with God and the way you speak to Him to be driven by problems and needs. God wants to be so much more to you than a quick fix.

Let me share a lesson with you I learnt a few years ago. In March 2009 I was diagnosed with Guillain Barré syndrome (you can read about this in my book *A Silent Adventure*). In this book, you will read about some of the extremely traumatic experiences I had while I was sick. Things were really not going well at all. As part of my recovery process, our family decided to spend some time together at the coast. However, our vacation started in the worst possible way, as I experienced a real setback and became ill again. In a moment of desperation, I called a friend and asked him to pray for me. I think I also wanted a bit of sympathy from him but his response was simply that I should begin to *praise* and *worship* the Lord – which of course was the last thing I felt like doing at the time. However, I decided to follow my friend's advice. I placed my joy in God and praised Him for His goodness and grace. The moment I became God-conscious and stopped focusing on my own needs and problems, my circumstances changed. My focus shifted away from myself and my own inability and I focused on God and His ability. I had forgotten that He had already rescued me from the depths of despair, but when I began to focus on praising and worshiping Him, my body began to heal supernaturally - so much so that I could actually begin to enjoy the time with my family. Healing took TIME – it wasn't an instant thing, but because I shifted my focus away from myself and instead focused on God, I could declare day in and day out that God is only good! In that moment I realized anew that God is faithful to fulfill His Word and the joy of the Lord, regardless of my circumstances, will always flow from my life.

I would like to share another example with you where I realized, once again, that the joy of the Lord needs to be my focus, and not my circumstances. One evening, I was going over a number of financial obligations that I had to attend to. One of my challenges was that I needed to pay the mortgage and our bank account did not have sufficient funds. It was late at night – and as you know, things often seem much worse when it's dark outside. In my case, this is exactly what happened. I looked at my circumstances and was gripped by fear. While I was considering all the things I would have to say to the bank manager the next day, I remembered the Word that I had confidently preached to our congregation for the past few Sundays. I got up right there and then, took my Bible and started to read from the Gospel of Mark. The more I read, the more I experienced the peace of God come over me and the joy of the Lord became my strength. Around 11pm that night, a friend of the family called to say that we were on her mind - she could not stop thinking about us. She asked me if everything was okay. It's not always easy to share your own crises with other people and so I initially decided not to share my financial situation with her. I soon realized, however, that this telephone call was no coincidence. She told me that she has wanted to sow into our ministry for quite some time now, and as a result she decided to deposit a large sum into my bank account right away. The fact that she wanted to deposit the money wasn't the only miracle – she happened to be a client at the very same bank as me, which meant that the funds were immediately available – there was no waiting period at all. I once again realized that God is good! You may have experienced similar situations and it is actually sad that we don't always remember the lesson that God is always good. Since that experience, I have found myself countless times depending on my own ability and insight, yet again – unfortunately I can't give testimonies of these as I am not particularly proud of these times. The question that you and I must answer is: WHOM will we trust? WHO is greater than my problems and my trials – my ability or God and His Almighty ability?

7
THE POWER OF MY WORDS

There is authority in the name of Jesus.

Have you noticed that when you're around friends or colleagues they often bring the name of a famous person into the conversation to add value to the point they're trying to make? As God's children, the Bible tells us we have the AUTHORITY to use the NAME of JESUS CHRIST in our everyday lives. In Philippians 2 we read:

> *Therefore God also has highly exalted Him and given Him the name which is above every name, that at the name of Jesus every knee should bow, of those in heaven, and of those on earth, and of those under the earth, and that every tongue should confess that Jesus Christ is Lord, to the glory of God the Father.* (Philippians 2:9-11, NKJV)

It is essential that we use His name. Doing so opens doors. It shifts and prepares heavenly resources for purposeful action. There are people who may use the names of Steve Jobs, Mark Shuttleworth or Bill Gates in order to win favor or to open doors, but we as believers have access to another NAME altogether. This is the Name ABOVE ALL NAMES, ABOVE ALL AUTHORITY, ABOVE

> **It is essential that we use His name. Doing so opens doors. It shifts and prepares heavenly resources for purposeful action.**

ALL DISEASE, and ABOVE ALL NATIONS. This Name has life, power and abundance. We have the Name of JESUS CHRIST, the Son of GOD! In Hebrews 1 we read:

[God] has in these last days spoken to us by His Son, whom He has appointed heir of all things, through whom also He made the worlds; who being the brightness of His glory and the express image of His person, and upholding all things by the word of His power, when He had by Himself purged our sins, sat down at the right hand of the Majesty on high, having become so much better than the angels, as He has by inheritance obtained a more excellent name than they. (Hebrews 1:2-4, NKJV)

My dear reader, whatever you are facing right now, call upon the **NAME ABOVE ALL NAMES – THE NAME OF JESUS CHRIST**. When you and I align our confession with the Word of God, He releases kingdom rule over our lives. Read these words from 2 Corinthians 4:7-15 in the Wuest translation:

But we have this treasure [the reflection of the light of the knowledge of the glory of God in the face of Christ] in earthenware containers, in order that the super-excellence of the power might be from God as a source and not from us.

We are being hard pressed from every side, but we are not hemmed in. We are bewildered, not knowing which way to turn, but not utterly destitute of possible measures or resources. *We are being persecuted, but not left in the lurch, not abandoned, not let down. We are being knocked down, but not destroyed, always bearing about in our body the dying of the Lord Jesus in order that the life of Jesus might be clearly and openly shown in our body, for, as for us, we who are living are perpetually being delivered over to death for Jesus' sake in order that the life of Jesus might be clearly and openly shown in our mortal body. So that death is operative in us* but the life is operative in you. But we have the same Spirit of faith *[as the Psalmist] according as it has been written and is at present on record, I believed, wherefore I spoke.* And as for us, we are believing, wherefore also we are speaking, *knowing that He who raised up the Lord Jesus shall also raise us with Jesus and shall present us with you, for all things are for your sake in order that the grace having been multiplied through the intermediate agency of the many [in their prayers for me] may cause the thanksgiving to super abound, resulting in the glory of God.* (2 Corinthians 4:7–15, WUEST Translation)

In 2 Corinthians 4:13 we read:

And since we have the same spirit of faith, according to what is written, "I believed and

therefore I spoke," we also believe and therefore
speak ... (2 Corinthians 4:13, NKJV)

Let's see how this passage of Scripture applies to our lives. Allow me to rephrase this passage from the Wuest translation into a confession:

I declare today in the name of Jesus Christ, the Name above all names, that:

- I have received the true treasure – that is, the knowledge of the glory of God.
- It is Christ in me.
- This source of Power and Life is God, the Origin and Source of all things.
- I declare, in the midst of the pressures of life around me, that nothing will prevent me from doing what God has purposed for me to do.
- I declare, in spite of the chaos around me, that my God is with me and I am not without help or Godly provision.
- I declare, in spite of persecution, that I am neither alone nor destitute: in fact, I am part of God's divine plan.
- I declare that the TRUE life is within me – Life that triumphed over death.
- Death is never the end; it is a seed that must give life.
- I declare, therefore, in the name of Jesus Christ that I BELIEVE, and therefore I speak.

In the Beginning was the Word

I've mentioned several times in this book that it is absolutely essential to have a personal relationship with Jesus. This relationship starts by having a daily relationship with His Word, because He is the Word. I realize that the Bible isn't JESUS, but the words written in the Bible have Life. I want to briefly explain the difference between the words *Logos* and *Rhema*. In English we only refer to "Word", while in the Greek there is a distinct difference between *Logos* and *Rhema* word. *Logos* is defined as a word (as to realize an idea), a declaration or a public speech. It appears 330 times in the New Testament with reference to a person who shares the message. *Logos* therefore refers to the entire inspired written Word of God, and it refers to Jesus. It is found in Scriptures such as John 1:1, Luke 8:11, Philippians 2:16 and Hebrews 4:12 to name a few. *Rhema*, on the other hand, is defined as something that is spoken, a word or a saying that is uttered; an order, report or promise. *Rhema* (the spoken word) is often used in the New Testament where reference is made to the Lord's dynamic, living spoken words that are uttered by a believer, or that are spoken in order to activate faith. Examples of *Rhema* can be found in verses such as Luke 1:38, 3:2 and 5:5, and Acts 11:16. I can also explain the difference by means of this simple example: If you open your Bible to Psalm 23 and read it, this is *Logos* – the written Word of God. When a particular verse from Psalm 23 stands out for you and you feel like God is saying something specific to you through the verse, then it is the *Rhema* word (the spoken Word of God). *Rhema* also refers to those times when you're waiting in line at the grocery store and God tells you to buy an extra loaf of bread for someone in need. When we read the Bible, we see that when God spoke, something came into being. This is how creation came into existence. There are countless examples in the Bible where God spoke and His Words made things happen. God did nothing without first speaking. If God places such immense value on words, how could we feel any different?

In the first chapter of the book of John we read:

In the beginning was the Word, and the Word was with God, and the Word was God. He was in

the beginning with God. All things were made through Him, and without Him nothing was made that was made. In Him was life, and the life was the light of men. And the Word became flesh and dwelt among us, and we beheld His glory, the glory as of the only begotten of the Father, full of grace and truth. (John 1:1-4, 14, NKJV)

Perhaps you've heard or read somewhere that your relationship with Jesus is not intimate enough? For many years, this idea was something of a mystery to me, just like the mustard seed we discussed in Chapter 5. How is it possible for me to love Him more, or to have more of Him in my life? Years later I discovered the answer, which is actually quite SIMPLE – get more of His Word in your life. His Word is a living seed that makes its home in our hearts, and which brings forth life. The Bible clearly states that His Word cannot return VOID – it must achieve the purpose for which it is sent. Luke 1:37 states:

For with God nothing will be impossible. (Luke 1:37, NKJV)

In the Concordant Literal New Testament the same verse reads like this:

It will not be impossible with God to fulfill every declaration.

If you ask me who Jesus is, my answer is that He is the WORD that was with GOD in the beginning of the HEAVENS and the EARTH. He was present during the process of CREATION. If I could rephrase John 1:1-4 and verse 14, it would look like this:

In the beginning was the Word (JESUS CHRIST), and the Word (JESUS CHRIST) was with God, and the Word (JESUS CHRIST) was God. He (JESUS CHRIST) was in the beginning with God. All things were made through Him (JESUS CHRIST), and without Him (JESUS CHRIST) nothing was made that was made. In Him (JESUS CHRIST) was life, and the life (JESUS CHRIST) was the light of men. And the Word (JESUS CHRIST) became flesh and dwelt among us, and we beheld His (JESUS CHRIST'S) glory, the glory as of the only begotten of the Father, full of grace and truth.

Everything came into being by the Word, in other words, through JESUS CHRIST. We can therefore, say this about HIS WORD:

- His Word is LIFE.
- His Word is AUTHORITY.
- His Word is IN CHARGE.
- His Word is the FUTURE.
- His Word SUSTAINS us.
- His Word brings a new WAY OF LIVING.

If I consider His Word and all that it contains, I know that I can BELIEVE HIM more than any politician, actor, singer, economist, philosopher or academic.

If I consider His Word and all that it contains, I know that I can BELIEVE HIM more than any politician, actor, singer, economist, philosopher or academic. I BELIEVE that I can trust JESUS CHRIST and HIS WORD with EVERYTHING IN ME. This is the reason why we need to read His Word. I need to memorize it and declare it. I don't declare Willem Nel's words, but the Word of JESUS CHRIST. Jesus declares in John 14 that He is the WAY, the

TRUTH and the LIFE.

What does the WORD says about the WORD, Jesus Christ?

In the beginning God created the heavens and the earth. (Genesis 1:1, NKJV)

God created the earth by speaking a WORD. God said, "Let there be Light"– that WORD was the SOURCE OF LIFE and that WORD IS JESUS CHRIST. Once, while I was busy preparing a sermon, I read the following commentary on Psalm 33:6 and Proverbs 8:30:

> *Jewish teachers emphasized that God had created all things through his Wisdom/Word/Law and sustained them because the righteous practiced the law. Some even pointed out that Gen. 1 declared "And God said," ten times when he was creating, and this meant that God created all things...*

And now, O Father, glorify Me together with Yourself, **with the glory which I had with You before the world was.** (John 17:5, NKJV)

What position did Jesus hold? What was His Glory that is spoken of here? The answer is that GOD CREATED THROUGH HIM.

In our pursuit to establish what the Word says about the Word, we also need to look at 1 John 1. There we read:

> ***That which was from the beginning, which we have heard, which we have seen with our eyes, which we have looked upon, and our hands have handled, concerning the Word of life - the life was manifested, and we have seen, and bear witness, and declare to you that eternal life which was with***

the Father and was manifested to us. (1 John 1:1, NKJV)

Once again, we see that JESUS CHRIST is the WORD, and that He is LIFE! HIS Word is ALIVE! I came across the following words which really struck me:

To the Jew a word was far more than a mere sound; it was something which had an independent existence and which actually did things. As Professor John Paterson puts it: 'The spoken word to the Hebrew was fearfully alive. ... It was a unit of energy charged with power. It flies like a bullet to its billet.

This is why I love rephrasing Scriptures into FAITH DECLARATIONS. There are many television personalities like Dr. Phil or Oprah who have often spoken beautiful words which we can share with people, but these words are not SPIRIT inspired and do not bring life.

In Colossians 1 and Hebrews 1 we read:

For by Him (JESUS CHRIST) all things were created that are in heaven and that are on earth, visible and invisible, whether thrones or dominions or principalities or powers. All things were created through Him and for Him. (Colossians 1:16, NKJV – parentheses mine)

[God]... has in these last days spoken to us by His Son (Jesus Christ), whom He has appointed heir of all things, through whom also He made the worlds. (Hebrews 1:2, NKJV – parentheses mine)

These Scriptures prove yet again that Jesus Christ is the LIVING WORD. You CAN AND MUST USE HIS CREATIVE POWER in your world, your economy, your workplace, and your body. Allow His Word CLOSE TO YOUR HEART and in your MOUTH. Fill your life with HIS Word and SEE WHAT HE DOES.

The words I speak will reveal whether or not I truly believe because you will recognize either faith or unbelief in my words.

You may have a really valid question when reading all this. How can we say we have a relationship with God or that we walk with God when our words sound no different from an unbeliever? Most people, even Christians, might think, "Whatever, they're just words." They are not "just words." WORDS have creative power. Amos 3:3 states:

Can two walk together, unless they are agreed? (Amos 3:3, NKJV)

In this verse, God asks us, "Will you walk with Me? Will you be My friend? Then you have to agree with Me. You're only in agreement with Me when your words and MY WORD say the same thing." I have personally been confronted with this truth over and over again, and each time I have had to confess that my words have not been IN LINE with HIS WORD.

In Hebrews 11 we read:

By faith Enoch was taken away so that he did not see death, "and was not found, because God had taken him"; for before he was taken he had this testimony, that he pleased God. (Hebrews 11:5, NKJV)

In some translations of the Bible we read that God was proud of him, and that he PLEASED God. Have you ever wondered why these things were said of Enoch? The answer is that Enoch's faith was always in line with God's Word. He carried nothing with him but God's Word.

The words I speak will reveal whether or not I truly believe because you will recognize either faith or unbelief in my words. Jesus told us with good reason that the mouth speaks from the overflow of the heart. In his book *Words That Move Mountains*, Don Gossett says the following:

> *To affirm is to make firm. An affirmation is a statement of truth that you make firm by repetition. Your faith becomes effective by acknowledging every good thing that is in you in Christ Jesus.*

Jesus told us with good reason that the mouth speaks from the overflow of the heart.

The Bible is full of POWER WORDS that effectively become active once you DECLARE them. The power of DECLARATION lies in the fact that it testifies to what has ALREADY happened and is now being CONFESSED by you and me. It is essential that we are passionate in our declarations. When our declarations sound timid and tired, we are not really prepared for what God wants to release to us.

Jesus Himself believed in the power of repetition. In Matthew 26 we read:

> **So He left them, went away again, and prayed the third time, saying the same words.** (Matthew 26:44, NKJV)

Declare these words with me right now:
> God is WHO HE SAYS HE IS
> I am who God says I am
> God can do what He says He can do
> I can do what GOD says I can do
> God has what He says He has
> I have what GOD says I have

(adapted from Don Gosset's book)

Let's declare further:
> This is a new day that the Lord has made.
> I declare His goodness over my family and myself.
> I am His beloved.
> I am His favorite.
> I will praise the name of the Lord and declare the greatness of His name.
> I am NOT ASHAMED OF THE GOSPEL OF JESUS CHRIST.
> I know that HE who is in me, is Greater that he who is in the world.

> HE is greater than: my sickness, *(name your sickness if you are currently suffering)*
>   my finances
>   my circumstances
>   my enemies
>   my misfortune
>   my family and friends
>   my past
>   my present
>   my future
>   the country's economy
>   my problems at work

my addiction *(drugs, alcohol, television, idols or anything else)*

Therefore I will say EVEN THOUGH I AM WEAK, HE MAKES ME STRONG

I stand in humility, strong and courageous, full of faith, and bold before the LORD.

Therefore, IF GOD IS FOR ME, WHO can be against me.

I DECLARE THE NAME OF JESUS CHRIST over my day, my family and my circumstances. HIS Name is above ALL names, ALL powers and ALL authorities. He gave me the POWER and the RIGHT to declare HIS NAME!

I am GOD'S CHILD.

I am GOD'S SON /DAUGHTER.

I am GOD'S ambassador.

I represent JESUS CHRIST and therefore I STAND IN HIS righteousness.

I have been forgiven by HIS great grace.

Therefore I do not have a spirit of FEAR, but of POWER, LOVE and a SOUND MIND.

I am ready to LISTEN.

I am ready to receive what GOD has planned for me.

My God provides ALL I NEED according to HIS RICHES.

My CALLING AND PURPOSE are sustained by the SOURCE of LIFE, and therefore, my health, finances and influence are in line with the Divine calling I received from God.

God is my righteousness.

I am in CHRIST JESUS.

I am a NEW CREATION in CHRIST JESUS.

I was MADE to be more than a conqueror in CHRIST JESUS.

I rule and reign with JESUS.

TODAY I am empowered with joy and wisdom BY HIS SPIRIT.

I make sure HIS WORD remains in my MOUTH and in my HEART

In previous chapters I've referred to Romans 10:8-10 a few times. Let's read it again:

> *But what does it say? "The word is near you, in your mouth and in your heart" (that is, the word of faith which we preach): that if you confess with your mouth the Lord Jesus and believe in your heart that God has raised Him from the dead, you will be saved. For with the heart one believes unto righteousness, and with the mouth confession is made unto salvation.* (Romans 10:8-10, NKJV)

We need to LISTEN CLOSELY to His Word because usually the best sermons we hear are those we preach to ourselves! When His Word comes OUT OF your mouth it means that the Word is in your heart. If you declare with your MOUTH that JESUS is LORD – in other words, that He is the WORD, the TRUTH and the LIFE, and if you believe with your heart that God raised Him from the dead, you will receive His freedom, salvation and provision. You will experience *Soteria*.

Verse 10 says, "WITH THE HEART ONE BELIEVES". Why is it important to believe with our hearts? Simply because the words we speak come from the overflow of our hearts. Therefore, our HEARTS must be filled with HIS promises, HIS voice and HIS Word, in order for our MOUTHS TO DECLARE SALVATION *(Soteria)*.

I want to share a few short testimonies with you, from my own life as well as a few others. These testimonies are about rings and wallets that were lost, and were eventually returned because in each case the people involved kept God's Word close to their heart. They believed and called back their belongings by faith:

Celesté's ring

My wife, Celesté, never takes off her wedding ring – with a few rare exceptions. On the rare occasion that she does take it off, she always places it on the bedside table in our bedroom. One evening when she looked for it, it had simply vanished. We looked for it together, but when we couldn't find it, we decided to wait until the following day so that our domestic worker could help us.

With the help of our domestic worker, we went through the entire house again. We emptied the contents of every single drawer and went through them with a fine-tooth comb. Earlier that month we had heard a sermon by Kobus van Rensburg where he spoke about things that had gone missing from his house and how he had trusted the Lord and declared that the Lord would send His angels to bring back what had been lost. So we also began to declare this over and over again. My faith was still growing in this area but Celesté kept declaring that the ring would return.

This is where the story gets interesting. After a whole MONTH of nothing happening, my faith was not exactly growing - it was actually dwindling. I finally contacted my insurance company to report the "disappearance" of the ring. They needed a case number, and so they sent someone over to our house. The man came on the Saturday morning and helped look for the ring. Yet again it was nowhere to be found, but Celesté's faith remained unshaken. On the Sunday morning I went to church early. Remember, an entire month had passed since the ring had disappeared. When Celesté got to church a short while later she showed me the ring, now on her finger. At first I did not register what I'd seen. She showed it to me again, and obviously my reaction was, "YOU GOT YOUR RING BACK – where was it?" She said when she got up that morning the ring was on the bedside table where we'd been looking for a whole month, right before her eyes. His angels had found it and returned it to us.

Joey's rings

A few years later, Joey, a woman from our church, asked Celesté to pray with her. Joey and her husband had gone on vacation to a game reserve. They stayed in a camping site and used the shared bathroom amenities. She had placed her wedding ring and other jewelry in her toiletry bag. There was a gold bracelet, her watch, engagement ring and wedding ring. The next morning when she opened her bag, the rings weren't there. Joey's brother and his wife went through the bag and all its contents with her, but the rings were not there. Joey said she didn't think she would ever get her rings back. They contacted the camp authorities and offered a reward should anyone find them. On the first Sunday back home, they prayed together with Celesté after the service and called back the rings. After six weeks (SIX WEEKS!) her daughter borrowed the same toiletry bag and when she opened it, all Joey's jewelry including her rings were inside. When Joey thinks back on these events today, she remains joyful and very grateful for God's goodness.

Miss Hantie's ring

Miss Hantie is my youngest son, D'ianrew's favorite kindergarten teacher. One day when Celesté fetched D'ianrew from school, she noticed that Miss Hantie looked quite sad. When she asked her what the problem was, Miss Hantie told her that a week ago she had lost her wedding ring and couldn't find it anywhere. She said everyone had been looking for it, especially the children. Celesté immediately shared the testimonies of her own ring as well as Joey's jewelry. They prayed about it straight away. Read carefully what happened next. The next morning when they came to school and opened the classroom door, one of the children said, "Miss Hantie, there's your ring! It's right there on the floor near the door!" Supernaturally returned!

My wallet

Earlier in the year while on sabbatical, in Ballito (a small coastal town), I forgot my wallet on the roof of the car. It must have fallen off when I drove out of the complex where I was staying. After I realized what had happened, I searched everywhere for it. Having remembered all the amazing testimonies from Celesté, Joey and Miss Hantie, I understood that I needed to ask the angels to return my wallet. I did my part – I searched for it and asked everyone around the complex if they had seen it. The security guard at the complex told me he hadn't seen it, despite being able to describe the wallet in detail. Two days later when I saw this man again and asked him if he was sure he hadn't by any chance seen it, his response was, "No Mr. Nel. I still haven't seen your wallet." I had never actually told him my name.

As you can see from my Facebook status below, I called my wallet back in faith!

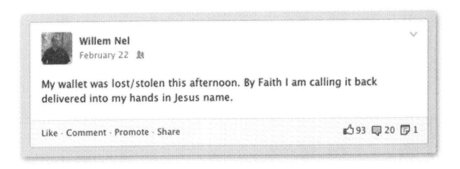

Willem Nel
February 22

My wallet was lost/stolen this afternoon. By Faith I am calling it back delivered into my hands in Jesus name.

Like · Comment · Promote · Share   93 20 1

On my last day there, I asked the security guard again if he had seen it. This time he asked for my telephone number and said, "No, Willem, I haven't seen it at all." I left it there and decided to forgive this guy. How could he possibly describe my wallet in such detail, and even know my name and surname?

When I got back home to Potchefstroom and was busy unpacking the car, I decided to continue trusting the Lord for my wallet's return. Two days later, a friend asked if I had found the wallet. My answer was, "No, I'm still trusting the Lord to send His angels to return it to me". I took my son D'ianrew to school and as I opened the car's passenger door, there it was – my wallet was just lying there, completely undamaged and nothing missing. Is it possible that it had fallen from the roof through the window? No, that would have been impossible because the window was closed when I lost it and we had thoroughly searched through the car many times. I have no doubt it was returned to me supernaturally! The next day I posted this message on Facebook:

Thank you Jesus! My wallet is back in my hand –

700km from where I lost it (Ballito). Thank you for all who prayed with me! I trusted God that His angels would return it into my hands. It is in my hands. When I lost it, it was on the car's roof on Saturday. I searched everywhere, but could not find it. But today (Friday morning) it was lying on the floor when I opened the passenger side of the car. It was not there earlier. God is faithful!

I want to use this opportunity to pray with you. Let's ask the Lord to send His angels to bring

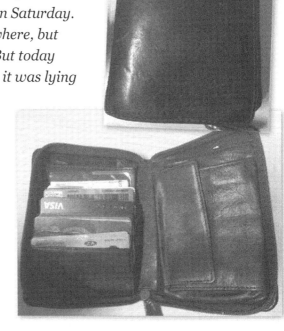

back what you have lost. Send us an email or a Facebook message when your things come back. GOD IS GOOD!

Remember to believe and to speak about His Word

There's a great deal of power in speaking about God's Word. Many sermons have been preached on believing God, but few have been preached on speaking about His Word. The Word of God is given to us in order to align our thoughts with Him or to straighten out our thinking. This means that His Word brings order to my natural thought process. Your faith will never be on a higher level than your thinking. The Bible clearly says that the Word will change your thinking. In Romans 10:10 we read:

> *For with the heart one believes unto righteousness, and with the mouth confession is made unto salvation.* (Romans 10:10, NKJV)

Sometimes your natural thought processes shift out of alignment with God's Word. You need to ask God to re-align your thoughts with His Word so that you don't pray against His will. What does it mean to pray against His will? I pray against His will if the Word of God does not dominate my prayer life. In other words, I pray what I think is right before seeking God's will. I've said many times that faith comes by hearing, and that hearing comes by the Word of God.

Your faith is only as effective as the level of your declaration. If you say you believe, but what comes out of your mouth is negative, your faith will not amount to anything. In Hebrews 4 we read:

> *Let us therefore be diligent to enter that rest, lest anyone fall according to the same example of disobedience. For the word of God is living and powerful, and sharper than any two-edged sword, piercing even to the division of soul and spirit, and of joints and marrow, and is a discerner of the thoughts and intents of the heart. And there is no creature hidden from His sight, but all things are naked and open to the eyes of Him to whom we must give account. Seeing then that we have a great High Priest who has passed*

through the heavens, Jesus the Son of God, let us hold fast our confession. (Hebrews 4:11-14, NKJV)

We need to pay careful attention to what we confess and according to this Scripture we need to hold onto our confession. This is important because:

- Our words bring life when they are in line with HIS Word.
- Our words must be a confession of HIS Word.
- It will cause the purposes of our heart to come alive.
- Faith will produce whatever it was called to achieve.

In Mark 11 we read:

So Jesus answered and said to them, "Have faith in God. For assuredly, I say to you, whoever says to this mountain, 'Be removed and be cast into the sea,' and does not doubt in his heart, but believes that those things he says will be done, he will have whatever he says. Therefore I say to you, whatever things you ask when you pray, believe that you receive them, and you will have them. (Mark 11:22-24, NKJV)

Jesus Himself taught His disciples to have FAITH in God. He is referring to the GOD-KIND of faith. It is an unshakable faith, free from doubt – a faith that stands firm on the truth. Regardless of our circumstances, we need to speak to every challenge. Even if it feels like you're facing an impossible situation, where there is no way out, you MUST speak to it and say, "Get out of my way!" Then you must believe that what you have spoken has already taken place, and that you have received your solution. This is when it becomes a reality in your life. I'd like to remind you of our faith process:

You allow His Word to come close to you

His Word is a light or a revelation to you

The light brings clarity or understanding (your mind understands the revelation)

When you understand you begin to trust

Trust gives you a place to stand

A place to stand gives you a platform

You must decide – will you act or remain passive?

I'd like to repeat this: faith aligns your thoughts with God's will and His will is the best for your life. I don't say this because it sounds like a neat statement. I understand the impact of words first-hand. I ended my book *A Silent Adventure* by saying that I did not know when I would preach or speak in public again. During the early days of my recovery process, my emotions were very unstable. My family found it difficult to cope and at times it actually became unbearable for them. Freedom came when I re-aligned my thoughts with God's Word and His will (which I still have to do regularly).

In 2010, as a family we began to minister all over the country. We shared my testimony about my illness wherever we went. I've mentioned earlier that my prognosis was that I would not speak again, and certainly never preach again. Subsequently through our ministry and specifically the testimony I shared, we have seen many miracles – deaf ears open, blind eyes being restored, people getting up out of wheelchairs, muscle tissue that grew back, heart diseases healed, and also financial breakthroughs for many people.

The enemy tried to destroy me through sickness and prevent me from preaching the good news, but God turned it into a platform. We shared our story with audiences ranging from a handful of people, to 20 000 people at one occasion. *A Silent Adventure* is now available in many countries, as well as in e-book format (www.faithstory.co.za). As a result of this testimony, we started a publishing company with the aim of 'Making God Famous by telling His story.' Meanwhile, this has become a platform for other authors like Alan Platt *(We Start At Finish)*, Bill Bennot *(Unstoppable Kingdom)* and various other men and women of God.

> **The enemy tried to destroy me through sickness and prevent me from preaching the good news, but God turned it into a platform.**

We constantly receive amazing testimonies from around the world from people who have been impacted by our story. Elizabeth Abdalla from Church of the King in USA emailed me this testimony:

Pastor Willem,

I just wanted to update you on what is going on in our lives. We so desperately want to visit and learn from you and your family but I am 21 weeks pregnant with our fourth child and if we visit you it would have to be now. Alas, airfare for our family would run upwards of

$8,000 and we do not have that, yet... Dan, my husband, will be visiting with Pastor Todd and the small group he is bringing at the end of July. I'm so excited for him to learn from you guys, the Lord is truly with you.

I don't know if you remember the first time you prayed with us, you prophesied that we would have five children and said that I would be pregnant by the next time you visited (I had just suffered a miscarriage). Well, I found out I was pregnant with Claire 2 weeks before your next visit. When you visited that time, you prayed over Claire (in my womb) and prophesied that the next baby would be a boy, that he would be known, and that people would write books about him. Well, baby boy Emory Louis will be joining us in October!! We found out on Thursday (though we really knew he was a boy all along). We picked his name because it means 'brave and powerful warrior' and we pray he will be a warrior for Christ.

More good news! We received a drilling plan in the mail this week! This is the next step to seeing this part of our prophecies fulfilled. They have proposed three wells on this one site, on our property! When you were here a few weeks ago you prayed that barriers and hindrances would be taken down and that this work would go forward. Well, here it is! I cannot wait to be able to tell our entire story to others. God has been so good to us! This video gives a little more of our story. (http://vimeo. com/30611812)

I just want to encourage you. I can only imagine how hard it is to be not only a pastor, but also a traveling minister. You are a blessing to us and to many others! Thank you for being willing to follow Jesus into all the places he leads!"

We are of the God kind, not the human kind

We are of the GOD KIND and not simply the HUMAN KIND. Every time my family and I share our testimony about my illness, this realization hits me once again, especially when Celesté shares from Psalm 103:1-5. This was the scripture she and the children held onto during my illness. I'd like to share it with you just like Celesté usually shares it with others. Read with me from the New King James Version:

We are of the GOD KIND.

Bless the Lord, O my soul; And all that is within me, bless His holy name! Bless the Lord, O my soul, **And forget not all His benefits:** *Who forgives all your iniquities, Who heals all your diseases,* **Who redeems your life from destruction,** *Who crowns you with loving-kindness and tender mercies,* **Who satisfies your mouth with good things,** *So that* **your youth is renewed like the eagle's.** (Psalm 103:1 - 5, NKJV)

I want to begin with the part that says, ***"and forget not all His benefits"***. When you fully understand and confess the **benefits** of the cross, you will see that His cross closed the door to all sin, every disease, and curse. There is no place for these things in your life anymore, and they no longer have any hold on you.

Then it says, **"who forgives all your iniquities"** – in other translations the words **"all your sins"** are used. The Lord took **ALL** your sin and unrighteousness upon Him and cancelled them at the cross. YOU and I can therefore come to His throne of grace, all because of HIS perfect and complete work on the cross.

We then read, **"who heals all your diseases"** – He [Jesus] took **all** diseases, pestilences, and viruses on Him, and RELEASED us from them. Disease therefore has no place in your body.

"Who redeems your life from destruction [curse]" He destroyed the CURSE at the CROSS. Our lives have been redeemed from all destruction. He cancelled all negative family patterns at the cross. Anything that tries to destroy your life has already been cancelled. He has completely **REDEEMED** us.

He did not simply remove or cancel the negative things, but His perfect work on the cross GAVE US THE FOLLOWING: He crowns us with HIS authority; He roots us in the FOUNDATION of His love *("Who crowns you with loving-kindness and tender mercies")*. Like the father in the parable of the Lost Son, He gives us His undeserved GOODNESS. He surrounds us with his FAVOR and LOVE. HIS LOVE gives us a new POSITION and PLATFORM.

> David, the Psalmist, wrote, "TASTE and SEE that the Lord is good".

He puts pleasant things in our mouths *("Who satisfies your mouth with good things")*. David, the Psalmist, wrote, "TASTE and SEE that the Lord is good". Do you know the expression, "He has tasted success?" The taste of success is the taste of HIS VICTORY IN YOUR MOUTH. Your mouth tends to be dry when you are tense or anxious or you may even have a bad taste in your mouth. The realization that HE FILLS US with PASSION and GOOD THINGS will bring a sweet taste to our mouth. When you taste this success, you will know you are standing in HIS PURPOSE – that His GOODNESS surrounds YOU.

"So that your youth is renewed like the eagle's" – HE RENEWS your POWER - SPIRIT, SOUL and BODY. It's like getting your youth and energy back. He restores your vitality. He RENEWS and RESTORES and RENOVATES it.

I have to say, after reflecting on Psalm 103:1-5, it's impossible to doubt we are of the GOD KIND!

Learn how to program yourself with the Word

The challenges you're currently experiencing are the DOOR TO PROMOTION that awaits you. See your sickness, your financial challenges, broken relationships or offenses as your promotion. Stand firm in your faith and program yourself with God's Word, because you will rise from the ashes of adversity. You will never attain greatness or be exceptional if you fight ordinary battles. An enemy is a necessity, as there will always be a Goliath, a Pharaoh, a satan who stands between you and what you are destined to become. You are not designed to fight ordinary battles. Program yourself with the Word of God!

Make sure that your thinking does not limit God. We limit God when we think too small. Have you ever said, "It's impossible – it can't happen to ME. I'm just an ordinary person." OH, NO – you're not ordinary, because you are of the GOD KIND. Great things can happen to you! We limit God when we are negative and say things like, "It won't happen to me. Nothing good has ever happened to me." We also limit God when we are driven to ACHIEVE and always try to FIT IN. In Romans 12:2 we read:

> ***And do not be conformed to this world, but be transformed by the renewing of your mind, that you may prove what is that good and acceptable and perfect will of God.*** (Romans 12:2, NKJV)

In the Phillips translation this verse reads as follows:

> ***Don't let the world around you squeeze you into its own mould, but let God re-mould your minds***

from within, so that you may prove in practice that the plan of God for you is good, meets all his demands and moves towards the goal of true maturity. (Romans 12:2, Phillips Translation)

Our thoughts are aligned with God by bringing our confession in line with His will and His Word. This verse in the Wuest Bible translation reads as follows:

And stop assuming an outward expression that does not come from within you and is not representative of what you are in your inner being but is patterned after this age; but change your outward expression to one that comes from within and is representative of your inner being, by the renewing of your mind, resulting in your putting to the test what is the will of God, the good and well-pleasing and complete will, and having found that it meets specifications, place your approval upon it.

Your behavior and especially your words need to be aligned with God. You need to see this reflected not only in your actions, but also in your facial expressions! Let's read Colossians 3:1-2 in The Message:

So if you're serious about living this new resurrection life with Christ, act like it. Pursue the things over which Christ presides. Don't shuffle along, eyes to the ground, absorbed with the things right in front of you. Look up, and be alert to what is going on around Christ—that's where the action is. See things from his perspective. (Colossians 3:1-2, The Message)

If you are serious about your life with Christ, ACT ACCORDING TO THE TRUTH! Apply the Word like it's a script for your life – learn the words, get into character and live your role effectively and SEE how circumstances around you change. The last sentence of this verse tells us to see things from Christ's perspective. This is so essential because HIS opinion carries a great deal more weight than my opinion. Let's talk about the Law of Gravity versus the Law of Aerodynamics. I can sit in an airplane with my hand luggage with me, and all my other bags neatly in the haul. But if there's no pilot, the plane won't get into the air. The pilot applies the Law of Aerodynamics to get the plane to take off. Say, for example, the engines fail in mid-flight. The Law of Gravity tells us that the chances of the plane falling are really huge. Where am I going with this this example? My confessions that have been aligned with God's Word are higher than the world's laws of suffering or disease. I do, however, need the pilot – Jesus Christ – and the Word in order to LIFT ME UP above the circumstances that are saying something else. Read these words from Romans 12:1-2 in The Message:

My confessions that have been aligned with God's Word are higher than the world's laws of suffering or disease.

So here's what I want you to do, God helping you: Take your everyday, ordinary life - your sleeping, eating, going-to-work, and walking-around life— and place it before God as an offering. Embracing what God does for you is the best thing you can do for him. Don't become so well adjusted to your culture that you fit into it without even thinking. Instead, fix your attention on God. You'll be changed from the inside out. Readily recognize what he wants from you, and quickly respond to it. Unlike the culture around you, always dragging you down to its level of immaturity, God brings the best out of you, develops well-formed maturity in you. (Romans 12:1-2, The Message)

Take your life, and place it before God as a living sacrifice. Don't allow our culture of reason and logic to convince you that God is not able to do what He says He can. HE IS ABLE!

After everything that has been said, the question remains, "How do you respond when faced with a crisis?" In his book *The Tongue, A Creative Force*, Charles Capps describes how some people can react in a particular situation (and I must admit I have been known to react like this at times). He uses the example of cars driving towards a crossing to make his point. According to Capps, we are like the driver approaching a crossing who anticipates another car approaching the same crossing from a few hundred yards away. Driver 1 realizes that if he accelerates, he will hit the other car and so he reacts based on what he thinks will happen. He can stop right where he is, in the middle of the road, but this could cause a major pile-up. In his mind, he still anticipates a particular scenario that determines his response. He doesn't realize that the other car has more than enough time to pass through the crossing without them crashing into each other. This is how we usually respond in times of crisis. Our response is often determined by what we think might happen. This kind of response means I am acting in unbelief. I often stop what I am doing simply to avoid something happening.

I need to adjust my unconscious mind and believe that I have more than enough time to make a decision because my thoughts are in line with Christ.

Some time ago, a friend called me to say he had received bad news about a family member. The doctors had given this person a death sentence. My friend had a choice. He could simply accept the doctor's report as the final verdict or he could seek God's opinion on the matter. He really didn't have to blindly accept this as the truth – he could get a second opinion or seek alternative treatment. Ask God for Wisdom. Ask the leaders of your church to pray with you, to lay hands on the person, and to bring the matter before God. We are quick to say, "This is the reality and these are the facts. And facts don't lie. The doctors say I'll never have a normal life." During my illness the TRUTH was greater than facts. FAITH in God said that I would speak across the whole world, even though I could not speak a single word at the time. If I constantly aligned my life with the realities around me, I would have caused a huge pile-up, because I would have stopped when I just needed to keep going. Psalm 91 has always been a source of light and truth in my life, even today. I want to conclude this chapter with this Psalm:

During my illness the TRUTH was greater than facts. FAITH in God said that I would speak across the whole world, even though I could not speak a single word at the time.

He who dwells in the secret place of the Most High
Shall abide under the shadow of the Almighty.

I will say of the LORD, "He is my refuge and my
fortress;
My God, in Him I will trust."
    Surely He shall deliver you from the snare of
the fowler
And from the perilous pestilence.
He shall cover you with His feathers,
And under His wings you shall take refuge;
His truth shall be your shield and buckler.
You shall not be afraid of the terror by night,
Nor of the arrow that flies by day,
Nor of the pestilence that walks in darkness,
    Nor of the destruction that lays waste at
noonday.
A thousand may fall at your side,
And ten thousand at your right hand;
But it shall not come near you.
Only with your eyes shall you look,
And see the reward of the wicked.
    Because you have made the LORD, who is my
refuge,
Even the Most High, your dwelling place,
No evil shall befall you,
    Nor shall any plague come near your
dwelling;
For He shall give His angels charge over you,
To keep you in all your ways.
In their hands they shall bear you up,
Lest you dash your foot against a stone.
You shall tread upon the lion and the cobra,
    The young lion and the serpent you shall
trample underfoot.

*"Because he has set his love upon Me, therefore
I will deliver him;
I will set him on high, because he has known
My name.
He shall call upon Me, and I will answer him;
I will be with him in trouble;
I will deliver him and honor him.
With long life I will satisfy him,
And show him My salvation.* (Psalm 91, NKJV)

There are so many powerful promises in this Scripture, and each one is a Godly declaration. Read verse 1 again. It says, *"He who dwells in the secret place of the Most High shall abide under the shadow of the Almighty"*. Verse 2 begins with the words, *"I will say of the LORD"*. Today people may regard you as arrogant if you made such a statement. "Who are you to do such a thing? Who gave you the right?" But if you and I want to see change in our lives and circumstances, we need to stop telling God how much we are suffering, and rather talk to God about what He has promised us. Repeat His Word over and over again. Declare His Word, speak His Word. During my illness I had to speak these words over my life repeatedly:

*Because he has set his love upon Me, therefore I
will deliver him;
I will set him on high, because he has known
My name.
He shall call upon Me, and I will answer him;
I will be with him in trouble;
I will deliver him and honor him.
With long life I will satisfy him,
And show him My salvation.* (Psalm 91:14-16, NKJV)

Someone once told me that when they were young, their dad would teach them about the importance of their words. Whenever they said anything negative about themselves, their ability or their future, he would reply with a little rhyme, "If you speak it, you'll reap it; if you confess it, you'll keep it."

Speak to the things that do not yet exist as if they did!

It was his light-hearted way of alerting them to the dangers of speaking negatively. They had the choice of either meeting their declarations in the future, or changing their words right then.

Whether you want to believe it or not, WORDS have power. Everything we see and experience on earth every day, God created with words. In the same way, your words have the power to create. Let's look at Isaiah 55:11 and 1 John 1:1 and 14:

So shall My word be that goes forth from My mouth;
It shall not return to Me void, But it shall accomplish what I please,
And it shall prosper in the thing for which I sent it. (Isaiah 55:11, NKJV)

In the beginning was the Word, and the Word was with God, and the Word was God ... And the Word became flesh and dwelt among us, and we beheld His glory, the glory as of the only begotten of the Father, full of grace and truth. (John 1:1, 14, NKJV)

REMEMBER:
- Our words have power.
- A Word brings faith.

- Faith brings righteousness.
- Righteousness gives us a place to stand before God.
- If we have a place to stand, we can speak!

Also remember these words from 2 Corinthians 4:

> *And since we have the same spirit of faith, according to what is written, "I believed and therefore I spoke," we also believe and therefore speak.* (2 Corinthians 4:13, NKJV)

Speak to the things that do not yet exist as if they did!

8
FAITH THIEVES

ONE OF THE GREATEST FAITH THIEVES of our age is FEAR. Although fear is no joke, I still want to start this chapter on a lighter note. I once read a story about a government official who set out to do an investigation into the circumstances surrounding a particular farm. The farmer warned this man that it would not be a good idea to carry out his investigation at that moment, but the official stuck to his guns and said that he certainly intended to do the investigation – and yes, it would need to be right NOW. Again, the farmer said, "You'd better not go into that enclosure", but the official ignored the farmer's warnings, saying, "I represent the government and I have a business card that allows me to enter any of these premises at any time, so I have the right to go in there." The farmer's response was, "Well, then go ahead, but it's at your own risk." The official arrogantly answered that he would not go in at his own risk but at the government's, because he has a card from them that permits him to do so. Not long after this, the farmer heard a terrible racket and saw the official running at great speed towards the gate, with fear all over his face. "Help! Help! Help!" he yelled, fearing for his life. There was an angry stud bull chasing him at full speed. Again, the official shouted to the farmer, terrified, "Help me! Please help me!" The farmer nonchalantly answered, "Just show him your card. You were pretty confident it could help you...I hope it does!"

The Lord has also given each of us a card. This card, however, is not like the one the official had. It's a powerful card that allows us to be anywhere, anytime, without fear. Many people may think, "I stopped being afraid long ago - I have no fear in my life". And yet, there are so many things that we fear (I will elaborate on these a little later), because the earth, our inheritance, is a dispensation of fear. In this chapter I want to share an important truth with you that I believe will change your life.

In the Bible we read the words that Paul spoke to Timothy. Timothy cried out to Paul, "Help! I don't want to be here anymore! I've had enough! I'm ready to throw in the towel". Timothy, however, had another problem. There was no way his cry for help would reach Paul fast enough and also no way that Paul's answer would get back to him in time. There were no computers to send an email or mobile phones to send a quick text message or make a call. It took months for Timothy to hear back from Paul. After several months, Paul wrote him the following words:

Therefore I remind you to stir up the gift of God, which is in you through the laying on of my hands. For God has not given us a spirit of fear, but of power and of love and of a sound mind.
(2 Timothy 1:6-7, NKJV)

In the Amplified Bible this verse reads as follows:

That is why I would remind you to stir up (rekindle the embers of, fan the flame of, and keep burning) the [gracious] gift of God, [the inner fire] that is in you by means of the laying on of my hands [with those of the elders at your ordination]. For God did not give us a spirit of timidity (of cowardice, of craven and cringing and fawning fear), but [He has given us a spirit] of power and of love and of calm and well-balanced mind and discipline and self-control. (2 Timothy 1:6-7, AMP)

Paul is saying to Timothy, "I know you're having a really hard time. You've got stomach problems and you need to drink some wine to help with that. I know your circumstances are terrible right now, but do you remember that time when we prayed for you? Do you remember when the fire of God came over you? Do you remember the anointing, the power and might you received from God? Timothy, do you remember? There's a fire within you that can break the power of the enemy – kindle that fire in your life again. Don't give up! Don't give in to fear!"

God has given us a sound mind, rational thinking and self-control. And yet it's precisely these things that often let us down and cause us to fear. The enemy always comes to you in the same way – he sows doubt and mistrust into your life. The enemy makes you doubt whether you're busy with the right things, whether you are really living a life of victory and whether you're good enough. Before long you find yourself in a pit – a hole so deep you doubt if you'll ever get out. The moment you start to doubt, the enemy is able to pin you down and paralyze you. Have you ever been stung by a wasp?

This is what the devil does – he wants to numb and paralyze you; he wants to discourage and derail you by sending things your way that will cause you to doubt.

If so, you'll remember the paralyzing numb feeling you get where you're stung. This is what the devil does – he wants to numb and paralyze you; he wants to discourage and derail you by sending things your way that will cause you to doubt. This is exactly what happened to Job. We read about this in Job 3:

> *For the thing I greatly feared has come upon me, and what I dreaded has happened to me.* (Job 3:25, NKJV)

Fear is the devil's faith and when I fear, I am putting my faith in the devil. I'm not talking about things that are reasonably frightening. It's obvious that you are careful when you cross the road and you're clearly looking for trouble if you play with snakes and spiders. I'm speaking of real fear – you're sitting in your house or room or you're driving in your car and suddenly you are caught in the grip of anxiety. You fear something, and this becomes such a reality to you that it feels as if it's right there with you. Perhaps someone said something to you that caused you to fear. Your marriage might be going through a rocky patch and your friend, who you invited round for coffee says, "Have you heard of my friend's friend whose mom got divorced after so many years?" In that moment an unknown fear grips you and you wonder if your marriage will make it. You may overhear someone saying, "Have you heard what's happening to the property market? It's bad! Buying a house as an investment right now would be an unwise decision..." – and that happened to be the day you just signed the papers for your new house. Worse yet is when someone comes to you saying, "Have you heard about that great Christian who served the Lord all his life? Well, he was robbed -they took everything and left him for dead..." and as fear grips you, all you can think is, "what could possibly happen to *me* then?"

I've mentioned previously in this book that fear – like faith – comes to you. Fear comes to you in the form of doubt and wreaks havoc in your mind. It feels like you need to take a few pills just to get rid of the jitters. Have you ever played that game with daisy petals where, as you pull off each petal you say, "he loves me, he loves me not?" Perhaps nine times out of ten it ended with "he loves me not". Fear makes you experience the negative side of life almost exclusively, just like the petal that tells you, "he loves me not".

As a group of leaders, we once made a list of typical things people feared. These are some of the things we came up with:

- People fear the future – will you get a job, will it be a good job, will you find a husband or wife and will your marriage work?
- Fear of commitment.
- Fear of failure – we are afraid things won't work out the way they should.
- Fear of being alone.
- Fear of death.
- Fear of God.

Fear brings doubt and mistrust, but God counters these things and brings life through His Spirit. Over the next few pages I will take you through the Word, because the Word brings TRUTH and LIGHT. What do I mean by this? Let me explain it this way: People sometimes start rumors and before long these stories are believed as the truth. Last year (2013) our honorable and beloved former president Nelson Mandela passed away. A few years before his death, a rumor was circulating that he had, in fact, already died. This rumor was accompanied by other reports of anarchy, revolution and even a race war. Suddenly many people were afraid – and I'm not talking about a mere case of the jitters - they felt real FEAR. A day or so after the rumors started, a newspaper printed a life-sized picture of Mr. Mandela on the front page showing him with his walking stick – alive and well at that stage. As quickly as the fear flared up, it was dispelled when the picture was published. What exactly happened here? The photo and the newspaper article gave people perspective regarding the truth. In the same way, I'd like to take you through the Word so that you will gain the right perspective. I specifically want to focus on the process Jesus went through at the time of His death. In Hebrews 4 we read these words:

For we do not have a High Priest who cannot sympathize with our weaknesses, but was in all points tempted as we are, yet without sin. (Hebrews 4:15, NKJV)

When Jesus Christ walked the earth, He was a human being in every sense. Although Jesus is the Son of God, He experienced exactly what you and I experience every day. Men, Jesus also had to fight against lust. Ladies, Jesus also had to work through various emotions. With all due respect, Jesus was not some sort of Superman when He was on earth – He was a human being in every way. Because He was fully human the Word says that He sympathizes with our weaknesses. After all, Jesus died for our sins.

The enemy – the devil – wasn't sure if Jesus really was the Son of God. There had been powerful men before Him, like Elijah and John the Baptist, so the devil had to make sure that Jesus was, indeed, the Messiah. He used every opportunity to try and stop what Jesus was doing and prevent Him from functioning. Yet, he still wasn't sure whether he was dealing with the true Messiah until the day of the crucifixion. I want to take you through the process of His death. In Luke 23 and Romans 10 we read:

And when Jesus had cried out with a loud voice, He said, "Father, 'into Your hands I commit My spirit.'" Having said this, He breathed His last. (Luke 23:46, NKJV)

... that if you confess with your mouth the Lord Jesus and believe in your heart that God has raised Him from the dead, you will be saved. (Romans 10:9, NKJV)

We don't like talking about death. Some people feel very uncomfortable and even a little frightened when you mention it. As a family, death came very close to us a few years ago when my dad and grandfather passed away within months of each other. There are times that I feel such a deep longing when I think of them, but I have come to realize that people don't even want to think about death, let alone talk about it. However, it's really important to understand the death of Jesus - not only His death but also His triumph over death, because it holds unprecedented power. Why is this important for us to understand? The Word says if you confess with your mouth that He is Lord, and believe with your heart that He was raised from the dead, you will be saved.

Jesus is hanging on the cross - broken, bleeding and crushed and yet he still shows grace to the man on His left by promising him that he will be with Him in paradise. Jesus is about to die and with His last breath he says, "My Father, You would never forsake me...why have You forsaken me?" Jesus gave His last breath, but He died with a Word that had been engraved on His heart. In Acts 2:24 we read:

... [Jesus] whom God raised up, having loosed the pains of death, because it was not possible that He should be held by it. (Acts 2:24, NKJV)

In some Bible translations such as the King James Version, we read that Jesus descended "into the *lower parts of the earth*" (meaning into hell). In other words, He entered Hades (the kingdom of death). Jesus died and He literally went to hell (Hades, also the place of torture), because He took all of our sins upon Himself. Can you see the picture? Jesus physically went to hell – He did not go to a sanctuary or a comfortable refuge. No - He was in the fiery pit because of your sins and mine. The enemy mocked and ridiculed Him, thinking he had finally won the battle over Jesus. I can imagine the enemy said something like, "Finally, I've got You. I hold the keys to Hades, and there's no way You're getting out of here". But when Jesus went into Hades, He carried a **Word** with Him. Peter speaks of this in his first sermon in Acts 2:25-28 where he quotes Psalm 16:8-11, a Psalm of David:

> *For David says concerning Him [Jesus Christ]:*
> *'I foresaw the LORD always before my face, for He is at my right hand, that I may not be shaken.*
>
> *Therefore my heart rejoiced, and my tongue was glad; moreover my flesh also will rest in hope.*
>
> **For You will not leave my soul in Hades** *[the kingdom of hell]*,
>
> **Nor will You allow Your Holy One to see corruption.**
>
> *You have made known to me the ways of life; You will make me full of joy in Your presence.'*
> (Acts 2:25–28, NKJV, parentheses mine)

He [Jesus] knew by this Word that God would raise Him from the dead. (Please read Psalms 16 and 22 for more on this).

Try to visualize the picture. God created hell (Hades) and satan has the keys – it's impossible to get out of there. This is not a maximum-security prison made by people. It was really IMPOSSIBLE to escape from there. Satan told Jesus, "Do you see that I've got the keys in my hands? I won't open the doors for you. This is your final outcome – you're going to suffer here forever". Jesus, however, didn't listen to him, because He entered Hades with a Word – we read in the Bible that He started preaching to the prisoners, his fellow citizens of hell. Jesus barely managed to speak out the Word in His pain and suffering and absolute desolation: "You will not leave me here in Hades, You will not allow Your Faithful Servant to perish."

Psalm 22 describes this moment as follows – I quote from The Message to capture the emotion:

You will not allow Your Faithful Servant to perish.

God, God ... my God! Why did you dump me miles from nowhere?

Doubled up with pain, I call to God all the day long. No answer. Nothing. I keep at it all night, tossing and turning.

And you! Are you indifferent, above it all, leaning back on the cushions of Israel's praise?

We know you were there for our parents: they cried for your help and you gave it;

they trusted and lived a good life. (Psalm 2:1-5)

I'm a bucket kicked over and spilled, every joint in my body has been pulled apart.

My heart is a blob of melted wax in my gut. I'm dry as a bone, my tongue black and swollen.
They have laid me out for burial in the dirt. (Psalm 22:14-15)

You, GOD—don't put off my rescue! Hurry and help me! (Psalm 22:19-20)

You can hear His desperation, but listen to how David prophetically describes what Jesus would say when in Hades:

I will proclaim your name to my brothers and sisters. I will praise you among your assembled people. (Psalm 22:2 NLT)

You see, when you hear God's Word and it starts coming alive in you, it becomes a reality to you. It drives out fear and you are able to take a stand and speak. This is exactly what Jesus did. In spite of His circumstances and the words of the enemy, He declared, "Father, You said that You will never leave Me. Lord, Your Word says that I will rise up out of this. Your Word says that I am an overcomer". Jesus began declaring the words of Psalm 16 and 22 repeatedly, and these are the words He preached in hell. The people around Him cried out as they were in pain and covered with wounds. In spite of Jesus' own pain and the wounds of His crushed body, He preached and He kept the Word close to Him. You can only preach if the Word is alive within you. Preaching is not simply taking a book and reading from it out loud. No! The words must be alive in your heart. Jesus had one Word – that His Father would deliver Him from hell (Hades) – and this is what He stood by. Jesus' circumstances told Him that it was IMPOSSIBLE – God made hell and He couldn't break His own rules by letting

Jesus escape through the back door.

    Something began stirring in Hades. The people started saying, "Keep preaching ... Tell us more. We want to hear more of what You have to say". While Jesus declared this Word and the Word came close to Him, the Word began to do the following:

Jesus let the Word come close to Him

The Word brought Him light, or revelation

The light brought clarity and understanding

Jesus understood and He began to trust, in other words, He believed

Faith or trust gave Jesus righteousness. "Father, I have the right; You said that I am the Son of God. I am the First. You will raise Me".

Righteousness gave Him a place to stand

Jesus had to decide whether He was going to act or remain passive. He acted – He started to speak, and when He spoke the Spirit of God began to move.

The Spirit of God cannot remain static when God's name is spoken. God cannot allow His Word to return void. Amid the impossibility of hell, in the impossibility of escaping from it, God's Spirit came and began to MOVE. Jesus preached to the captives in hell and to everyone who was in Hades. David wasn't in hell, but he was, however, in Hades, in a place of safekeeping. Jesus preached to everyone and the Spirit of God came like a wind and opened the doors of hell so that Jesus could lead the prisoners into freedom. It wasn't really a case of Jesus going to hell, remaining there for three days and then being set free. No, it was a place where He had to keep the Word close to Him. That's why the Bible says in Romans 10:9 -

... that if you confess with your mouth the Lord Jesus and believe in your heart that God has raised Him from the dead, you will be saved. (NKJV)

The word "saved" here is the Greek word *Soteria* that means to experience God's favor, His peace, His glory, power and majesty in **every** area of your life – not only in certain areas or just one area, but in **each and every area**. God **wants** to bless you abundantly.

A few years ago, four armed men attacked two pastors in our congregation, Louise Buys and Fiona Matier, in the house they shared. Read with me how Louise testifies about the events of that night (Fiona's testimony also appears later in this chapter):

It was just after dark on the evening of 29 October 2010. It was lovely outside and the smoke from barbeques was visible everywhere in the neighborhood. I went in and out of the house, and took the hosepipe to the swimming pool to fill it up. I planned to leave the hose on for another 5 or 10 minutes and then I was going to lock up. Fiona, my housemate, was on the phone with her mom. While I was waiting, I was watching the television program 'Noot vir Noot' (a South African music quiz program) and was also busy texting a friend to wish her a happy birthday.

While I was busy texting, something caught my eye and when I looked up, I looked straight into the barrels of revolvers held by four young men who stood in my front door like uninvited guests. I got such a fright – on the one hand it felt as if everything inside me froze, and at the same time a zillion thoughts rushed through my mind.

My first thoughts were: Why on earth didn't I lock the door when it got dark? Why have I never thought about some sort of emergency plan? Things like this only happen to other people...Serves me right. Couldn't I just have thought of...? Where is God with His promise of protection? Why do angels exist if none of them are at their posts when you really need them? We're in big trouble.

But then, once you come to your senses, your mind is filled with the deposit you've made over months and years – a deposit that has become your faith. That night, what filled my mind after the initial shock, was not something I heard in one sermon or something I wrote down in my notebook one day. I am fortunate to say that my faith is not based on the things we read in the newspapers every day that scare so many people. My mind was on **God's** thoughts about me, that have been invested in me over the years and which I chose to believe.

"Shift the battlefield; you are loaded with weapons in the spirit realm!"

One of the men pressed his gun to my chest, and I realized that I was defenseless. I didn't have a firearm to use against them but I heard in my spirit God speaking to me, saying "Shift the battlefield; you are loaded with weapons in the spirit realm!" I remembered that our battle is not against flesh and blood, but against the evil spirits that controlled these men like puppets. I remembered that Pastor Willem Nel always *taught us to act and function according to that which is true in the realm of the spirit and not according to the things we see or experience in the physical dimension around us.*

In my spirit I knew that God loved me, that He has rooted and grounded me in His love so that when I am faced with life's storms (or guns), I will remain standing, like a great oak tree.

...That Christ may dwell in your hearts through faith; that you, being rooted and grounded in love. (Ephesians 3:17-20, NKJV)

I remembered that Jesus carried all the punishment I deserved and that there would be no reason why He would want to punish me or hold me accountable for anything in this terrifying way.

Therefore, as through one man's offense judgment came to all men, resulting in condemnation, even so through one Man's righteous act the free gift came to all men, resulting in justification of life. *(Romans 5:18 NKJV)*

I remembered that I am an heir in His will and testament. This testament contains no clause about break-ins! On the contrary it states that He has forgiven my sins, healed me from disease, saved me from destruction, crowned me with His love and goodness, and that He has seated me with Christ in heavenly places where I rule with Him.

A few days before the break-in, Pastor Cindi Lombardo said something to me completely out of the blue over dinner that I remembered in that moment. She took a spoonful of dessert and said "Sweetie, always remember, when you pray in tongues, you confuse the enemy".

It was time to take a stand and act according to what I could see in the spirit – and confuse the enemy!

One of the men grabbed me from my chair. I looked him straight in the eye and began to pray out loud in tongues. Fiona looked at them and loudly declared the Scripture that had been up against our refrigerator for the last couple of months: "NO WEAPON FORMED AGAINST US SHALL PROSPER, you will not take our lives."

The men tied us up in a bedroom and we decided to act like Paul and Silas and praise the Lord until this prison door opened. You must know that if you are locked up in a room with a Worship Leader and your life is in danger, you will certainly end up praising the Lord. Worship, or "strength" according to Psalm 8, is something God places in the mouths of infants in order to silence the enemy. After three minutes the house was silent. My greatest loss was my Blackberry.

Soon the trauma of the experience set in and we had to process the effect it had on our bodies, but in our hearts we experienced the sweet taste of victory – a victory that God had accomplished for us in the spirit. In this intensely traumatic moment I experienced what Jesus meant when He said, **"I say to you, whoever says to this mountain, 'Be removed and be cast into the sea,' and does not doubt in his heart, but believes that those things he says will be done, he will have whatever he says."** *And* **"whatever things you ask in prayer, believing, you will receive."**

You may be facing a crisis at this point in your life – a pit that feels like hell, and you don't know the way out. You may be anxious and full of fear, feeling like "what if I never get out of here"? I'm not trying to undermine what you're going through or make it out to be nothing, but you are definitely not in hell where there is no way out. Jesus Christ, our Lord and Master, who was in hell Himself, says that the way out is to take the Word of God and to preach it to yourself over and over again. When you speak God's Word over your circumstances and your fears, you release His power and you will begin to see and experience this power in your life.

At this point I'd like to share Fiona's testimony about that "fearful" night. You will notice that I put the word fearful in inverted commas, because when you read Fiona's testimony, you will see that fear was not the major role-player in this story. Fiona writes:

It had been a really peaceful day. My friend, Louise and I had spent the day being pampered at a Spa and I remember a conversation we had shared there about feeling so grateful for God's peace. We really felt His presence with us and we were literally basking in it the whole day.

Little did we know how this peaceful day would turn out ...

If I remember correctly, it was somewhere between 7 and 8pm. It was a beautiful summer's evening, and I was chatting to my mom on the landline and Louise was sitting in the lounge sending a text message. The front door was open – we often left the door open during summer, as we would sit outside regularly. Actually, I think Louise was busy watering the garden, and she was about to go outside to switch off the taps.

While I was on the phone, I looked up and suddenly saw

four men walk through the front door. It was so surreal. My first thought was, "Do we know them? Are they people we know from church?" And then I saw the guns and the knife and realized these were not invited guests. One of the men pointed a gun directly at Louise's chest and another man held a huge knife against her from behind. She let out a scream and tried to kick the guy holding the gun to her!

Another man came up to me and ripped the phone out my hand and threw it to the floor. In that moment, I literally felt everything stand still. I felt the most incredible peace surround me, and a boldness rising up inside. I looked directly at the man pointing the gun at me and said, "No weapon formed against us shall prosper. You will not take our lives." This is not something I thought about – it just came out of me. Interestingly, this was the scripture that had been on our refrigerator the past couple of weeks that we read every day. He then pushed me down on the ground and held a gun to the back of my head. I could hear Louise praying loudly in tongues, I could feel the man's hand shaking as he held the gun behind my head. I remember saying to him, "Don't worry, it's going to be all right. Everything is going to be ok." And I just kept saying, "No weapon formed against us shall prosper."

The guys were confused. They started arguing with each other and shouting at each other. They kept asking us where the safe was, but we don't have one and the more we said we don't have one, the more they argued with each other. Later that night when it was all over, Louise told me that she remembered a friend telling her just that week that when we pray in tongues we confuse the plans of the enemy. Well, that night we experienced it first hand.

I felt the presence of Jesus with me that night like

I have never felt in my entire life. I knew He was right there and I knew we were going to live. The guys ended up taking us to my bedroom and tying our hands together with electronic cabling – a camera charger and a phone charger I think. They locked us in the bedroom while they presumably carried on looking for stuff to steal. They weren't the brightest criminals because they ended up tying my hands together in front, so I could easily untie myself and help Louise.

Before they left the bedroom, I looked one of them directly in the eyes and said, **"Don't worry. Jesus really loves you. He really loves you guys."** *And that was the last we saw of them.*

"Don't worry. Jesus really loves you. He really loves you guys."

We were stuck in my bedroom without any cellphone or any means of getting out. So we looked at each other and decided to begin to praise God! It was our very own Paul and Silas in the prison moment...they sang praises to God in their midnight hour and the Lord delivered them, so we were going to do the same! We sang and praised God and prayed for the men.

It was literally a few minutes later that we noticed the house was very quiet and the guys must have left. We were alone, and still stuck in my bedroom. Grateful to be alive and completely unharmed, we began to giggle and realized the only way out was to shout for help. So we began calling out in the hope that a neighbor would hear us and come to our rescue. We must have shouted for a good fifteen minutes before anyone actually responded.

We phoned our good friends Franci and Dieter Jordaan

who were there in absolutely no time at all. After they arrived, I don't remember much – they pretty much took care of everything. I remember so many people from our church coming over to see if we were all right and helping in various practical ways. What an absolute blessing to be a part of a Spiritual Family and for friends who help when it matters the most.

The men ended up stealing my Apple computer and both of our Blackberry phones, but if I think about what could have happened, I am so grateful to God for His presence, His protection and the confidence we had in Him that "greater is He that is in me that he that is in the world." That day, those men thought they were in control. They thought their weapons gave them authority and I'm pretty sure they expected us to just scream, panic and give in to them. But that day, they encountered true spiritual authority for the first time and it made them panic. We were in control, not them. Not because we are so amazing, but because in that moment, we knew that God was with us and His presence in us was greater than what we were facing in the physical realm.

That day will go down in my book of life as an amazing day! It was a day where the Word of God was victorious, and His presence a powerful reality. Louise and I prayed for the salvation of those four men and I wish I could see them again to ask them what they experienced that day, because I am convinced that they saw Jesus, right there in our house with us.

I can imagine there are some of you feeling a chill in your spine as you read this, especially if you're a woman. Two vulnerable, young, unarmed women against four strong, armed young men. The only thing Jesus had when He entered Hades was a Word - a Word that His Father would not forsake Him. Louise and Fiona also had a Word in their moment of "hell" – a Word that no weapon formed against them would prosper. They knew God had good plans for them in mind and this is what they began to declare (just as Jesus preached). The Spirit of God cannot remain unmoved when His name is glorified – He begins to move and blow like a wind, and just like He did for Jesus, Louise and Fiona's "prison door" was blown open by the Spirit. Yes, they lost their mobile phones and a computer, but they walked triumphantly out of their "hell"! Due to the Word of God in them, there was no room for fear and they could even declare His love to their enemies!

There is a portion of Acts 2:24 where we read about Jesus being *"raised up, having loosed the pains of death"*. The word loosed here means that Jesus destroyed it. The dictionary defines the word 'loosed' us untied or freed. Due to the fact that it was impossible for Jesus to be held captive by death, He took its key and loosed or unlocked it. Why was it impossible for hell to hold Him down? Simply because Jesus had a Word! While He was in hell, He didn't have a Bible or a verse with Him, there was no minister or pastor who could quickly pray for Him, or someone He could text – He had nothing but a Word from God, a promise from God (which was also the case with Louise and Fiona. They could not ask the armed robbers if they could quickly look up a suitable verse in the Bible. God's Word was close to them and therefore they could speak it with confidence). The promise came to life and it loosed, broke off, and completely destroyed the power of darkness!

Peter wrote these words in Acts 2:27:

For You will not leave my soul in Hades, nor will You allow Your Holy One to see corruption. (Acts 2:27, NKJV)

With these words Peter is actually saying, "Lord, You will not leave my soul alone. You will not give me over to death. I will not remain here because Your Word says that I will not be left to the powers of darkness". Right now I would like to ask you to begin to cry out to God, regardless of your circumstances. It doesn't matter how deep the pit is that you're in. It's time to stop casting blame and to stand up and follow the Master. Paul wrote these words in Ephesians 5:

> ***Therefore be imitators of God as dear children.*** (Ephesians 5:1, NKJV)

The words we speak sustain us – are they going to be words of life or words of fear?

Today, Paul is asking you and me to start doing what Jesus did. The words we speak sustain us – are they going to be words of life or words of fear?

In 1 Corinthians 2 we read these compelling words:

> ***But we speak the wisdom of God in a mystery, the hidden wisdom which God ordained before the ages for our glory, which none of the rulers of this age knew; for had they known, they would not have crucified the Lord of glory.*** (1 Corinthians 2:7-8, NKJV)

Paul is saying that if the enemy, who nailed Jesus to the cross knew the effect it would have, they would never have killed Him. It's about time for the enemy (satan) to understand that the things he attacks us with so often will have no effect, especially if we keep God's Word close to us. That's when we can literally deliver the knockout punch! In the Garden of Eden, Adam and Eve ate from the forbidden fruit. When God came to them, He asked Eve what she had done. She denied everything outright and blamed it on the serpent. God then asked Adam what he had done, and in turn he blamed it on the woman – neither of them actually took responsibility. God asked Adam and Eve, but He never asked the serpent. He told him immediately that he would crawl on his belly and eat dust. God does not negotiate with the devil, He does not give him the opportunity to speak and make excuses – no, He immediately sends him on his way. This is precisely what we should do when the devil comes to us – when he brings doubt, uncertainty and fear into our lives. Don't negotiate with him; speak him out of your life. We often do the opposite, however. The moment you say things like, "Nothing ever works out for me" or "We [add your family name here] are a sorry bunch - none of us will ever amount to anything," you are actually inviting the devil into your life. In fact, you're offering him refreshments and making sure he feels right at home. NO. This has to stop somewhere and it stops with a Word. When you receive bad news about your business, or about your job, about a disease or any other area of life, don't start negotiating with the devil – call a friend immediately, ask him or her to pray with you about the issue – to trust together with you for a Word from God. Begin to speak God's Word and His promises over your circumstances. It doesn't help to speak the negative things people are saying over your circumstances – it will not change your situation and it may, in fact, fill you with a greater sense of fear.

When Jesus entered hell, He had nothing. There were no angels with Him, and neither was God's power with Him – He was beaten down, or rather, He was literally beaten to a pulp. There was nothing left to motivate Him. All that remained was for Him to give up, but He did not surrender – because He had a Word.

Fear leads to distorted thinking. The word fear stands for:

F = False
E = Evidence
A = Appears
R = Real

The words "what if" are often connected to fear. "What if I don't make it?" or "What if I can't pay my bills?" or "What if I don't get healed?" While He was in hell, Jesus never, for one moment, asked, "What if I can't get out of here?" No, He knew He would get out of there, because He had a Word. In Ephesians 1:17-20 we read the following:

> *... that the God of our Lord Jesus Christ, the Father of glory, may give to you the spirit of wisdom and revelation in the knowledge of Him, the eyes of your understanding being enlightened; that you may know what is the hope of His calling, what are the riches of the glory of His inheritance in the saints, and what is the exceeding greatness of His power toward us who believe,* **according to the working of His mighty power which He worked in Christ when He raised Him from the dead** *and seated Him at His right hand in the heavenly places.* (Ephesians 1:17-20, NKJV)

Jesus knew! This reminds me of the animated film *The Lion King*. When the animals spoke the name "Mufasa", everyone trembled – whether it was Scar or the silly hyenas who heard it, they trembled. The devil trembles just like that when you speak the name of Jesus over your circumstances. **Jesus the King of kings; Jesus the Lord of Hosts; Jesus our Banner; Jesus the Name who is stronger and sharper than any double-edged sword.**

Your words will either sustain the enemy's place in your life, or your words will enable you to walk with Jesus in victory. When you act in faith, you admire God but when you act in fear, you admire satan.

You may be asking right now, "Willem, what do I do now? Where do I begin to get rid of fear?"

Begin by allowing the Word of God in your life, every day.

Read it, write it down and meditate on it. In James 1 we read:

> *... and receive with meekness the implanted word, which is able to save your souls.* (James 1:21b, NKJV)

The Greek word used here for "save" is *sozo*, which does not mean to get you into heaven, but to heal you, to make you whole. The Word is therefore able to heal you from your fear. Gary Player, the world-famous South African golfer, once said, "The more I practice, the luckier I get." In James 1:25 we read:

> *But if you look carefully into the perfect law that sets you free, and if you do what it says and don't forget what you heard, then God will bless you for doing it.* (James 1:25; NLT)

The speed at which the Word works in your

Your words will either sustain the enemy's place in your life, or your words will enable you to walk with Jesus in victory.

life is determined by the time you spend in it. An athlete cannot pitch up for a race if he has not trained for it – he can't expect to achieve any kind of success. In the same way, you and I can't successfully take part in the race of life without exercising our spiritual muscles, or our faith muscles, through the Word. To have the Word in your life is not a good idea – it's a ***PRIORITY***.

> **When you act in faith, you admire God but when you act in fear, you admire satan.**

The second thing we can do is to allow love in our lives.

In 1 John 4:18 we read:

> *There is no fear in love; but perfect love casts out fear, because fear involves torment.* (1 John 4:18a, NKJV)

Why is this so? Love reflects your origin (where you come from) and fear attacks this origin. Do you think the enemy is really interested in destroying your marriage, your finances, or your business? Do you think he wants to send a few accidents your way in order to teach you a lesson or two? We look for the devil around every corner, saying, "The devil wants to destroy my marriage". You need to understand that this is only the end result of what he's actually busy doing – he wants to destroy your sense of origin, because he knows you were born of God. Your spirit inside you knows that you were born of God. Your origin is God; you will not just live with God for eternity one day – you have lived with God for eternity. That is where you originate. You don't have a beginning and you don't have an end. You are an eternal being with God – you were born of God and you walk with God. If satan succeeds in destroying that origin in you through fear, he can paralyze you. This is when fear begins to take over your life – being fearful of the Lord, fearing finances, fearing marriage or other relationships.

The way to restore this fear is through love, because love is the origin or source. God is love, and you were born of God because of love. In Isaiah 43 we read these words:

> *But now, thus says the LORD, who created you, O Jacob, and He who formed you, O Israel:*
> *"Fear not, for I have redeemed you; I have called you by your name;*
> *You are Mine.... Since you were precious in My sight, you have been honored,*
> *And I have loved you; therefore I will give men for you, and people for your life.*
> *Fear not, for I am with you; I will bring your descendants from the east,*
> *and gather you from the west.* (Isaiah 43:1, 4-5, NKJV)

Thirdly, surrender yourself to the Spirit.

The Father is the Creator, the Son is the Word and the Spirit is the Dynamo – He is the power through which our world is governed and controlled. The head of the Kingdom of God on earth is the Holy Spirit. The Holy Spirit is here and wants to reign in your life. He wants to take control of your life. Subject yourself to the Spirit. In Acts 10 and Ephesians 1 we read:

> *... how God anointed Jesus of Nazareth with the Holy Spirit and with power.* (Acts 10:38, NKJV)

> *... and what is the exceeding greatness of His power toward us who believe, according to the*

working of His mighty power which He worked in Christ when He raised Him from the dead. (Ephesians 1:19-20, NKJV)

The same Jesus, the same power that raised Him from the grave, the very same power is present in you – all you have to do is to subject yourself to it. You need to surrender yourself and say, "I will allow the Holy Spirit to seal me." The word 'seal' that we read of in Ephesians means I have been stamped with the Father's stamp, the Father's mark of ownership is on me and I am preserved and protected by the powerful working of the Holy Spirit.

In Luke 12:32 we read:

Do not fear, little flock, for it is your Father's good pleasure to give you the kingdom. (Luke 12:32, NKJV)

The Lord tells us that because it was His great pleasure to give us the Kingdom, He sent His Spirit and that Spirit is inside us. We did not receive a spirit of fear, but a Spirit who calls out Abba Father – calling out to our origin. The Lord says, "Even if you walk through a valley of death, if you act from my Spirit, you will not fear any evil, because although I don't remove the shadow of death – it is on this earth – if you are in Me and your spirit is in Me and My Word is in you, you will fear no evil. You will walk out of the valley, empowered and by the power of the Holy Spirit's work in you, you will be completely fearless."

Lastly, allow the PEACE of GOD to guard your heart, and become a peace-maker.

Live in peace. Romans 14:17 declares the following:

Right thinking = Joy + Peace in the Holy Spirit.

For the kingdom of God is not eating and drinking, but righteousness and peace and joy in the Holy Spirit. (Romans 14:17, NKJV)

The life of faith (the Kingdom of God) is not about what we eat or drink, where we live or what we own – it's about our position – the Righteousness that was given to us by Jesus Christ. It's about Peace and Joy in the Holy Spirit. When you FEAR, your mind, will and emotions are attacked. This usually happens when you lose your Joy in the Lord and eventually you also lose the GUARD of PEACE guarding your mind and heart. If we were to represent this as a mathematical equation, it would look like this:

Right thinking = Joy + Peace in the Holy Spirit

However, when fear enters the picture, the equation looks like this:

Wrong thinking = Fear

The principle of PEACE is probably the most important principle I can teach in this book. When Celesté and I were once on vacation, someone gave her a few books to take along to read while we were away – one of them was *Living in Peace* by Joyce Meyer. Celesté and I used to be quite proud of both having strong opinions – and it didn't bother us to voice these differences of opinion, even in public. Perhaps given my political background, I was headstrong and stubborn, and I thought it was pretty cool to be that way. Celesté read this Joyce Meyer book and gave it to me to read the next day. It changed our lives completely. We realized that the Lord guards our lives with His peace that transcends all understanding. Peace is something tangible, like car keys - if you misplace them you need to retrace your steps in order to retrieve them. This principle of "living in peace" caused me, my family as well as the leaders of our church to constantly challenge each other to GUARD THE PEACE. Read with me what the Word says about this:

Peace is like a security guard in our lives. It can also be described as the DOOR of our house that keeps the beautiful promises and provision of God inside.

> *Pursue peace with all people, and holiness, without which no one will see the Lord: looking carefully lest anyone fall short of the grace of God; lest any root of bitterness springing up cause trouble, and by this many become defiled ...* (Hebrews 12:14-15, NKJV)

If people do not have peace in their lives, they become resentful and bitter. PEACE and HOLINESS speak of maturity in Christ.

Peace is like a security guard in our lives. It can also be described as the DOOR of our house that keeps the beautiful promises and provision of God inside. Let's read a few versions of Philippians 4:7 so that you can see clearly what I mean. In the New King James Version, it reads like this:

> *And the peace of God, which surpasses all understanding, will guard your hearts and minds through Christ Jesus.* (Philippians 4:7, NKJV)

The peace of God is much greater than the human mind can understand. This peace will keep your hearts and minds through Christ Jesus. (NLV)

Then you will experience God's peace, which exceeds anything we can understand. His peace will guard your hearts and minds as you live in Christ Jesus. (NLT)

And God's peace [shall be yours, that tranquil state of a soul assured of its salvation through Christ, and so fearing nothing from God and being content with its earthly lot of whatever sort that is, that peace], which transcends all understanding, shall garrison and mount guard over your hearts and minds in Christ Jesus. (AMP)

Why is living a life of peace and joy so important? It allows us to live in **unity** and **harmony**. In Philippians 2 we read the following words:

fulfill my joy by being like-minded, having the same love, being of one accord, of one mind. Let nothing be done through selfish ambition or conceit, but in lowliness of mind let each esteem others better than himself. Let each of you look out not only for his own interests, but also for the interests of others. Let this mind be in you which was also in Christ Jesus. (Philippians 2:2-5, NKJV)

I've already mentioned that it is love that drives out fear. Therefore, when we are like-minded in love, living in unity of heart and vision, the enemy cannot gain a foothold to deposit fear into our lives.

A life of peace and joy causes you to put your own agendas aside. It makes you seek God's plan for your life through prayer. It urges you to seek **HIS** way to live. Read with me these words from Acts 4:

> *So when they heard that, they raised their voice to God with one accord and said: "Lord, You are God, who made heaven and earth and the sea, and all that is in them.* (Acts 4:24, NKJV)

In Acts 13:22 we see that God looks for those who want to carry out HIS WILL:

> *And when He had removed him, He raised up for them David as king, to whom also He gave testimony and said, 'I have found David the son of Jesse, a man after My own heart,* who will do all My will'. (Acts 13:22, NKJV)

A life of peace and joy also means to live in the Spirit:

> *for you are still carnal. For where there are envy, strife, and divisions among you, are you not carnal and behaving like mere men?* (1 Corinthians 3:3, NKJV)

A life of peace and joy gives us a sense of unity so that we avoid strife at all times:

> *I, therefore, the prisoner of the Lord, beseech you to walk worthy of the calling with which you were*

called, with all lowliness and gentleness, with longsuffering, bearing with one another in love, endeavoring to keep the unity of the Spirit in the bond of peace. (Ephesians 4:1-3, NKJV)

Jesus also prayed and asked the Father that we would function in unity:

"I do not pray for these alone, but also for those who will believe in Me through their word; that they all may be one, as You, Father, are in Me, and I in You; that they also may be one in Us, that the world may believe that You sent Me." (John 17:20-21; NKJV)

The opposite of peace and joy is strife, discord and dissension. Both peace and strife are spirits. Both the atmosphere between people and the attitudes of people are influenced by peace and strife. Both peace and strife can be felt. Strife is defined as bickering, being argumentative, expressing differences in opinion and speaking in an angry tone. Why is it important to deal with the issue of "strife" in a chapter entitled Faith Thieves? Strife brings discord and it drives out love. I've noted that love is your origin, it is where you come from and if the enemy can attack this by means of strife, he will certainly do so. It may sound strange, but strife can lead to fear because it makes you doubt people's motives and integrity. A lack of trust affects your ability to think clearly, and according to our equation, wrong thinking = fear. In 1 Corinthians 1 we read how Paul makes an appeal not to tolerate strife among us:

God is faithful, by whom you were called into the fellowship of His Son, Jesus Christ our Lord. Now I plead with you, brethren, by the name of our Lord Jesus Christ, that you all speak the same thing, and that there be no divisions among you, but that you be perfectly joined together in the same mind and in the same judgment. For it has been declared to me concerning you, my brethren, by those of Chloe's household, that there are contentions among you. (1 Corinthians 1:9-11, NKVJ)

Where there is unity, there is blessing and anointing:

A Song of Ascents. Of David. Behold, how good and how pleasant it is for brethren to dwell together in unity! It is like the precious oil upon the head, running down on the beard, the beard of Aaron, running down on the edge of his garments. It is like the dew of Hermon, descending upon the mountains of Zion; for there the LORD commanded the blessing— Life forevermore. (Psalm 133:1-3, NKJV)

Where there is unity, GOD COMMANDS HIS BLESSING

In Genesis 13 we read that both Abraham and Lot were very wealthy. Abraham was blessed in an exceptional measure because he knew how to the keep strife out of his life. When a situation arose that resulted in a lack of unity between his herdsmen and those of Lot, he gave Lot the opportunity to choose the land he wanted because Abraham did not want to allow any discord in his life.

In Proverbs, Solomon also strongly advocates against strife:

Better is a dry morsel with quietness, than a house full of feasting with strife. (Proverbs 17:1, NKJV)

A perverse man sows strife, and a whisperer separates the best of friends. (Proverbs 16:28, NKJV)

He who covers a transgression seeks love, but he who repeats a matter separates friends. (Proverbs 17:9, NKJV)

I've already mentioned that strife is destructive. Not only should individuals avoid strife, but the church should also guard against it. In Hebrews 12:14-15 we read:

Pursue peace with all people, *and holiness, without which no one will see the Lord: looking carefully lest anyone fall short of the grace of God; lest any root of bitterness springing up cause trouble, and by this many become defiled* ... (Hebrews 12:14-15, NKJV)

Strife grieves the Holy Spirit:

And do not grieve the Holy Spirit of God, by whom you were sealed for the day of redemption. Let all bitterness, wrath, anger, clamor, and evil speaking be put away from you, with all malice. And be kind to one another, tenderhearted, forgiving one another, even as God in Christ forgave you. (Ephesians 4:30-32, NKJV)

Strife destroys your health. Read James 3:13-18 carefully with me:

Who is wise and understanding among you? Let him show by good conduct that his works are done

in the meekness of wisdom. *But if you have bitter envy and self-seeking in your hearts, do not boast and lie against the truth. This wisdom does not descend from above, but is earthly, sensual, demonic. For where envy and self-seeking exist, confusion and every evil thing are there. But the wisdom that is from above is first pure, then peaceable, gentle, willing to yield, full of mercy and good fruits, without partiality and without hypocrisy. Now the fruit of righteousness is sown in peace by those who make peace.* (James 3:13-18, NKJV)

Strife also causes doubt and as I've said, doubt gives rise to fear. What can we do about strife? What are we challenged to do? Francois du Toit, in his book entitled DONE, has the following to say:

> Our individual lives celebrate the fact that God reconciled the world to Himself. He brought hostility to an end. We are entrusted with a commission to bring about world peace! We will make war cease to the ends of the earth! The challenge, "to love your enemies and to do good to those who hate and abuse you" is no longer a far-fetched sentiment; it is the reality of our lives! We understand that "we wrestle NOT against flesh and blood" which means that a fellow man can never again be our target! God is man's friend and not his foe. The symptoms of imperfection, sin or sickness in a person do not make of the person the enemy.

The nature of my work requires me to travel a great deal. Although these times away are not always pleasant for my family or me, we find there is great joy when I return home. The children know there's always a surprise, no matter how small, from Dad. There's always something special for them. When I walk in the front door I usually listen to the goings on inside the house – excited to share what I have brought for them. Unfortunately, there have been times where I have returned home to find the kids quarrelling (not that often, thankfully). Hearing them fight with each other makes me put away their surprise for later, before I even greet them. I wait until the peace has been restored so that they will be ready to receive what I have to give them. I wholeheartedly believe the Word that says if we ask something in HIS name, we will receive. But when we fear or when we allow strife into our lives, I believe it is difficult for the Lord to release what He has prepared for us into that environment filled with fear and discontent.

We defeat fear when we live lives that others look up to and admire. In fact, Jesus said the peacemakers are blessed, because they will be called the SONS of God. Read with me from the Amplified version:

> **Blessed *(enjoying enviable happiness, spiritually prosperous–with life-joy and satisfaction in God's favor and salvation, regardless of their outward conditions) are the* makers and maintainers of peace, *for they shall be called the* sons of God!** (Matthew 5:9, AMP)

9
FAITH AND PATIENCE

IF YOU'RE LIKE ME, you like it when things happen quickly! Perhaps you're really excited about something you've read and want IMMEDIATE results. The Lord has challenged me about this way of thinking and is teaching me His process. I am learning to be patient and to wait for His leading. I know myself – I often get impatient quickly, when facing a giant (a difficult situation). How do you respond when facing something that feels impossible to you? Your giant may be a serious sickness, a financial crisis, an emotional upheaval, a lifelong dream that just doesn't seem to materialize, or poor self-esteem. When we face these kinds of difficulties, we need both FAITH and PATIENCE. In Hebrews we read:

> *And we desire that each one of you show the same diligence to the full assurance of hope until the end that you do not become sluggish, but imitate those who through faith and patience inherit the promises.* (Hebrews 6:11-12, NKJV)

Our FAITH and PATIENCE ensure that we don't miss out on God's promises. I think I've probably been on the brink of many breakthroughs in my life, yet missed them. Almost like the Israelites of old who threw away their promise just days before they would have reached the Promised Land, I have been so close to my breakthrough several times, but instead relied on my own insight or followed the ungodly opinions of others. Sometimes I've listened to the opinions of "Christians" – people who call themselves Christian but don't really believe God or trust Him. This has made me turn around and choose the safety of the wilderness, or the place I am used to, rather than taking the risk to FOLLOW God and take Him at His Word. Let's read this same verse in the Message and Mirror translations:

> *Don't drag your feet. Be like those who stay the course* **with committed faith** *and then get everything promised to them.* (Hebrews 6:12, The Message)

> *We do not want you to behave like illegitimate children, unsure of your share in the inheritance. Mimic the faith of those who through* **their patience** *came to possess the promise of their allotted portion.* (Hebrews 6:12, The Mirror)

We need to assess our behavior. How do we act? In the previous chapters, we see that our actions and words truly reflect our hearts. Our words and actions reveal whether we have chosen to make Jesus the High Priest of His Word.

Do you remember what Colossians 3:1 says? I quote again from The Message:

> *So if you're serious about living this new resurrection life with Christ,* **act like it.** *Pursue the*

things over which Christ presides. Don't shuffle along, eyes to the ground, absorbed with the things right in front of you. **Look up, and be alert to what is going on around Christ -** *that's where the action is. See things from his perspective.* (Colossians 3:1, The Message)

If we are really serious about this new life in Christ, our words and deeds need to show it! We need to make sure we ask ourselves the following before we act:

- What is HIS perspective on the matter; in other words, how does HE see it?
- What does HE say about our lives?
- What does HE say about our families?
- What does HE say about our bodies?
- What does HE say about the circumstances you and I are facing?

Perhaps you are overweight right now (or at least it feels like that to you), perhaps you are underpaid, you're deep in debt and it feels like nobody understands you. There may be many situations you feel you've got no control over but this is not the time to give up. There IS a winner inside of you! In fact, you are MORE than a conqueror. God made you to be the head, not the tail. Rise up! Be strong and courageous. Take your Bible and declare His goodness and favor. Don't give up hope – that's exactly what the enemy wants you to do. Come to His throne of Grace. Make Him the High Priest of your words, and HOLD ON! I repeat - don't give up hope.

> **There IS a winner inside of you! In fact, you are MORE than a conqueror.**

DIS–COURAGE is a word that consists of two parts - meaning to withdraw courage from you, to steal your courage or make you feel like you have no courage.

Do you remember the prayer of Jabez? His mother named him Jabez as an expression of her own pain and discomfort. Read these words from 1 Chronicles 4:

Now Jabez was more honorable than his brothers, and his mother called his name Jabez, saying, "Because I bore him in pain." And Jabez called on the God of Israel saying, "Oh, that You would bless me indeed, and enlarge my territory, that Your hand would be with me, and that You would keep me from evil, that I may not cause pain!" *So God granted him what he requested.* (1 Chronicles 4:9-10, NKJV)

The name Jabez literally means pain, sadness and difficulty. It must be terrible to go through life with a name like that. Imagine each time your mom calls you, she shouts, "Pain, sadness, difficulty, come over here!" What a name! But Jabez actually prays against the meaning of his name - he asks:

- Lord, bless me.
- Lord, enlarge my territory.
- Lord, keep evil and pain far away from me.
- Lord, keep Your hand over me – in other words, let me represent You instead of a person who couldn't even give me a good name.

This prayer of Jabez helps me each day to have faith and patience in an absolutely good God and His Word. Jabez turned away from the overwhelmingly negative meaning of his name and what it represented. The enemy will also try and stop you in your tracks, just like he tried to do with Jabez's name. He will try to discourage you! DIS–COURAGE is a word that consists of two parts - meaning to withdraw courage from you, to steal your courage or make you feel like you have no courage. Again, I want to encourage you not to flinch or draw back from your promise for one moment.

> **Again, I want to encourage you not to flinch or draw back from your promise for one moment.**

Don't Flinch

In Hebrews 10:35-38 we read:

> *Therefore do not cast away your confidence, which has great reward.* (Hebrews 10:35, NKJV)

This verse literally says we must not give up trusting in a good God because we will be rewarded for holding on. This reward is referring to the battle that has been completed and won. Think about it - in a sports game, the halftime score is only an indication of what the final score could be. The halftime score is never the determining factor of who will go on to actually win the game. So often we see the halftime score turned around just moments before the game ends. The players know they can never give up before the final whistle. In the same way I want to encourage you to keep going and never give up before the battle is won. A friend of mine once called me in great excitement. A transaction that we'd prayed for together eight years ago suddenly went through that day. The contracts were signed and the money was significantly more than it would have been eight years ago when we prayed about it. He could have easily given up hope, wondering if he'd ever clinch the deal. From a human perspective, nobody would blame him if he had stopped believing this transaction would go through – but he didn't. He held onto hope and trusted God – and he received his reward!

> *For you have need of endurance, so that after you have done the will of God, you may receive the promise.* (Hebrews 10:36, NKJV)

The Word says you need endurance. The dictionary describes the word endure as "to keep going to the end; to hold out against; to sustain without impairment or yielding." You need perseverance. You need to stick to the plan. Trust God, accept His goodness. Rejoice in the midst of the difficulty you are facing, because as you praise God and continue to declare His Word you will see the breakthrough!

> *For yet a little while, and He who is coming will come and will not tarry.* (Hebrews 10:37, NKJV)

God's timing is always perfect!

> *Now the just shall live by faith; but if anyone draws back, My soul has no pleasure in him.* (Hebrews 10:38, NKJV)

This might sound harsh – but if you draw back and are uncertain about what God has promised, you are what James refers to as a double-minded person who cannot expect to receive anything from God. Elijah is a good example of a Biblical prophet who did not flinch. You can read his story in the book of 1 Kings. Drought had caused a great famine in the land because King Ahab and his family had sinned against the Lord. They worshipped the idol named Baal and deceived all the people of Israel to do the same. In 1 Kings 18 we read the specific account of how Elijah received a word from the Lord that the drought was about to come to an end. It goes on to describe how both Elijah and the prophets of Baal prepared and offering, each to their god and how Elijah ended up making fun of the prophets of Baal because after a whole day of begging and pleading, Baal had not answered any of their prayers. Elijah, on the other hand, asked that his offering first be soaked with water and we read that after he prayed to the Lord, the Lord sent a fire that consumed everything – the animal sacrifice, the wood, the stones and even all the water. After the prophets of Baal had been killed, Elijah told Ahab to go and have something to eat, because he could hear the sound of rain approaching.

Allow me to quickly interrupt myself here. Imagine this scenario for a moment – drought had consumed this land for three and a half years. There was nothing – I mean, literally nothing. The land was an empty, dusty plane. There was not a cloud to be seen, but Elijah said he heard rain coming. After he said these words, he climbed to the top of Mount Carmel and rested with his head between his knees. Read with me from 1 Kings 18:43:

> *... and [Elijah] said to his servant, "Go up now, look toward the sea." So he went up and looked, and said, "There is nothing." And seven times he said, "Go again."* (1 Kings 18:43, NKJV)

Elijah had a clear Word from God, went to the king in faith and said all the right things – in other words, he complied with all the "requirements". When he sent his servant to see if any clouds had begun to gather, however, there was nothing. If I had been there, my response to the king after the servant had failed to see any clouds for the third time might have been something like this: "I'm sorry, I must have got it wrong. The rain isn't coming today after all – perhaps it will come tomorrow? You know the weather forecast is never very reliable." Just as well Elijah was there and not me – he never gave up hope. He knew that God's Word does not change! He sent his servant out seven times to look for a sign of rain. In the following verse of this passage we read:

Then it came to pass the seventh time, that he said, "There is a cloud, as small as a man's hand, rising out of the sea!" So he said, "Go up, say to Ahab, 'Prepare your chariot, and go down before the rain stops you'."
(1 Kings 18:44, NKJV)

What you are saying is IMPOSSIBLE, but God turned the impossible into the possible.

Make a fist with your hand, and look at it. That's how big the cloud was in the expanse of sky – it's difficult to imagine even being able to see such a small cloud in the sky, but it was enough for Elijah. He knew God had kept His promise. The odds were stacked against Elijah. Reality shouted out, "What you are saying is IMPOSSIBLE!" but Elijah stood firm in his faith and God turned the impossible into the possible. It is essential for us to trust God patiently UNTIL the breakthrough comes, because it will surely come. James teaches us that the waiting period tests our faith, and in the process develops patience. Sometimes we are so close to a breakthrough, but our impatience cancels God's promise, or postpones it. It's with good reason that we read these words in Romans 5:

> *And not only that, but we also glory in tribulations,*
> *knowing that tribulation produces perseverance;*
> *and perseverance, character; and character, hope.*
> *Now hope does not disappoint, because the love of*
> *God has been poured out in our hearts by the Holy*
> *Spirit who was given to us.* (Romans 5: 3-5, NKJV)

Abraham is an example of someone who ran out of patience. In the midst of God's process he decided to make his own plan. That plan's name was Ishmael. Please understand, there was nothing wrong with the boy, Ishmael - but the Ishmael plan that Abraham and Sarah came up with was wrong. If you make a plan from the flesh you will have to live with the consequences. God's plan for them was Isaac, not Ishmael. You and I need to learn to wait patiently for God's plan for our lives – and not make our own "Ishmael-plans".

Remember God's Miracles

It's easy to feel overwhelmed by our emotions and to fill our minds with all the world's problems. In the parable of the sower in Mark 4, Jesus tells us that the living seed of the Word can be stolen from us – this is exactly what happens if we allow our minds to be filled with the cares of the world. In 2 Peter 1:3 we read:

> **... His divine power has given to us all things that**
> **pertain to life and godliness, *through the knowledge***
> ***of Him who called us by glory and virtue.*** (2 Peter
> 1:3, NKJV)

In Christ Jesus, we have received everything we need to live a Godly life. He has called us to receive His glory and goodness! God's Word confirms this – whether or not I feel like it. God cannot lie. Read with me:

God is not a man, that He should lie, nor a son of man, that He should repent. Has He said, and will He not do? (Numbers 23:19, NKJV)

In 1 Peter 1:4 - 5 we read:

Now we live with great expectation, and we have a priceless inheritance—an inheritance that is kept in heaven for you, pure and undefiled, beyond the reach of change and decay. And through your faith, God is protecting you by his power until you receive this salvation, which is ready to be revealed on the last day for all to see. (1 Peter 1:4-5, NLT)

We are not only free – we also have the ability to escape the corruption of the world through HIS SUPERNATURAL NATURE.

We have been set free. We are no longer on the path of destruction or decay. In 2 Peter 1 we read this wonderful truth:

These are the promises that enable you to share his divine nature and escape the world's corruption caused by human desires. (2 Peter 1:4, NLT)

We are not only free – we also have the ability to escape the corruption of the world through HIS SUPERNATURAL NATURE. What makes it possible for us to escape? KNOWLEDGE (in other words, an intimate KNOWING) HIS Divine Power and Divine Nature.

Look at how Peter describes the process:

In view of all this, make every effort to respond to God's promises. *Supplement your faith with a generous provision of moral excellence, and moral excellence with knowledge, and knowledge with self-control, and self-control with patient endurance, and patient endurance with godliness, and godliness with brotherly affection, and brotherly affection with love for everyone.* (2 Peter 1:5-7, NLT)

By this time you probably know our process of faith. I want to draw your attention to it once more:

Let His Word come close to you

His Word is a light or a revelation to you

The light brings clarity or understanding (your mind understands the revelation)

When you understand you begin to trust

Trust gives you a place to stand

A place to stand gives you a platform

You must decide – will you act or remain passive? Your obedience to the Word that brings light will proceed into action [a deed]. This is a calculated risk that you take, because your trust is in a good and faithful God. Passivity will make you procrastinate and eventually it will make you give up!

We need to do everything we can to SHOW that we BELIEVE – in other words, our thoughts and actions must be in LINE with God's Word if we want to see these promises fulfilled. We BELIEVE because we know these promises have already been given to us. By declaring them, we have a PLACE TO STAND where we can act in accordance with the Word.

If we continue reading 2 Peter 1, we see the following:

The more you grow like this, the more productive and useful you will be in your knowledge of our Lord Jesus Christ. But those who fail to develop in this way are shortsighted or blind, forgetting that they have been cleansed from their old sins. So, dear brothers and sisters, work hard to prove that you really are among those God has called and chosen. Do these things, and you will never fall away. (2 Peter 1:8-10, NLT)

We need to work hard to prove that God has called us. Am I talking about physical hard work or our good deeds? No. We need to work hard on our faith declarations and our dependency on HEARING His voice. When we follow Him despite difficult circumstances, we prove that he has called us – we live our faith. Looking back, I remember when we first started talking about our desire to bring transformation to our city. We experienced a great deal of opposition from various sources. One thing that was really taboo in Potchefstroom at that time was having multi-cultural church services. My eldest son was dedicated to the Lord in 1995 by my friend, Pastor Anthony Constance, a man of color. The management of the church denomination I belonged to at that time tried everything in their power to remove me as pastor. One of our church members, Frieda Kishi, was the first black student to be awarded a leadership position on the university campus. Frieda was the first black committee member of her University residence management team. This all took place in Potchefstroom in the early 1990s.

I remember another situation where one of our student's parents contributed generously to our ministry. One day she "called me in" to inform me that her father was going to withdraw his support if I didn't stop this "ministry to blacks". I remember this like it was yesterday. I was able to confidently tell her that neither she nor her father took care of me – God called us and He would take care of us. For a few months our finances did not look great because her father, as well as others he had influenced, had withdrawn their support, but we stood firm on the Word of God. There was another case where a farmer from our region used to give us a great deal of financial support during the early 1990s. For a young campus preacher, this support was like manna from heaven. One day he took me aside and told me that he "really wanted to bless us". However, he had a condition – we had to stop our multi-cultural ministry and only minister to white students. We decided to get by without his contributions, rather than giving in to his demands, despite this having a significant impact on our pockets. Faith in God means that you stand for what is right, not for what is comfortable in the moment.

If we read further in 2 Peter 1, it says the following:

> *So, dear brothers and sisters, work hard to prove that you really are among those God has called and chosen. Do these things, and you will never fall away. Then God will give you a grand entrance into the eternal Kingdom of our Lord and Savior Jesus Christ. Therefore, I will always remind you about these things—even though you already*

know them and are standing firm in the truth you have been taught. And it is only right that I should keep on reminding you as long as I live. For our Lord Jesus Christ has shown me that I must soon leave this earthly life, so I will work hard to make sure you always remember these things after I am gone. (2 Peter 1:10-15, NLT)

Three times Peter tells us that he wants us to remember what he said. The price of righteousness and grace *brings good news that the world simply cannot resist*. This happens when we don't treat the people around us as enemies but we know that the sweet aroma spread by our faith will allow others to CHOOSE. That's when we can wave the Name of JESUS over their lives and their circumstances, like a banner. This is not far-fetched, or something we would expect to find in a Children's Bible Story. It's the reality of the GOOD NEWS. It is essential therefore, that we do what is written in Romans 12:2 – and I quote from the Phillips Translation:

Don't let the world around you squeeze you into its own mould, but let God remould your minds from within, so that you may prove for yourselves that the plan of God is good, meets all his demands and moves towards the goal of true maturity. (Romans 12:2, Phillips)

So don't allow the world to pressure you into conforming to its ungodly standards. Bill Johnson wrote these words: "Unbelief has the outward appearance of a conservative approach to life, but works to subject God Himself to the mind and control of people."

Patience and Longsuffering

I mentioned previously that I was diagnosed with Guillain Barré syndrome in 2009. This was initially extremely frustrating because so many specialists around me could not figure out what was wrong with me. After they eventually diagnosed me, all the negative prognoses followed – for example, that I would never preach again. Fortunately, I chose to believe God's Word rather than their negative prognoses. During my recovery process that lasted a few months, I often complained to God and my family. I felt really sorry for myself. Remember, I was senior pastor of a growing congregation, and now I'd become a person who could barely speak – all because of Guillain Barré syndrome. During this recovery time, the words in Galatians 5:22 became more than just words to me – I needed to live them each day. Galatians 5:22 tells us:

> *But the fruit of the Spirit is love, joy, peace, longsuffering, kindness, goodness, faithfulness.*
> (Galatians 5:22 , NKJV)

In the Living Bible this verse reads as follows:

> *... but when the Holy Spirit controls our lives he will produce this kind of fruit in us: love, joy, peace, patience, kindness, goodness, faithfulness.*

Have you heard this verse somewhere, or perhaps read it yourself? I'm sure you have. I've also read it, but I didn't really understand the patience and longsuffering that Paul spoke of. As my body was not immune to viruses or infections while I was recovering, I had to take endless courses of antibiotics after I was discharged from hospital. I also mentioned before that we decided to go on vacation while I was recovering as we felt it would help my body recuperate. Once we reached our holiday destination, however, I fell ill again. I developed a high fever and stayed in bed for three days. The worst part was that my entire family also got sick. In times like these you really want to blame somebody - you want to accuse someone for causing all the pain and misery. It was during this time that I had a revelation of what the word LONGSUFFERING meant. Steve Farrar writes:

> *Without the sovereignty and providence of God, you will always remain a victim. But when you discover the truth of these attributes of your heavenly Father, it throws the events of your life into a completely different light.*

I began to see longsuffering, which is a fruit of the Spirit, in a whole new light.

Definition of LONGSUFFERING

The Hebrew expressions *erek* and *aph* literally mean, "long of nose" or "long of breathing". Anger often goes hand in hand with quick, heavy breathing through the nostrils, which is possibly where these translations come from that speak of a person being "long of anger" or "slow to wrath", describing their "longsuffering". In the King James Version, God is described as being "slow to anger". In my case, longsuffering meant that I needed to hold my breath and not react out of anger or frustration. The Greek word *makrothymia* literally means "long of spirit or rage" – and it specifically refers to God's patience with sinners and the fact that He is slow to judge them. We can clearly see this in Romans 2:4:

Or are you [so blind as to] trifle with and presume upon and despise and underestimate the wealth of His kindness and forbearance and longsuffering

patience? Are you unmindful or actually ignorant [of the fact] that God's kindness is intended to lead you to repent (to change your mind and inner man to accept God's will)? (Romans 2:4, AMP)

J. Horst made this statement in his book *Makrothymia*:

Since it is a quality of God, it is also a fruit of the presence, guidance and enabling of the Holy Spirit in the believer (Gal 5:22) aiding him to endure trials and to be patient.

The purpose of God's longsuffering is, therefore, to lead people to salvation (repentance) and confession. It was God's purpose with me, and most likely with you too. Repentance means to change your mind and your thoughts completely. It means that you will begin to think differently about things. God does not make us sick, but through my circumstances I understood that God not only wanted to teach me what LONGSUFFERING meant, but also to live it.

Understanding Grace and LONGSUFFERING

The writer and theologian John once told his congregation in England: "*Some providences of God, like Hebrew letters, are best understood backwards*". In most Western languages we read and write from left to right. The Hebrew language, however, is read from right to left. Flavel argued that you might sometimes feel as if life is being read to you back to front. God's sovereignty and His provision might make no sense to you at any given point until you reach the end of that particular chapter or journey in your life. For me, my journey [my illness] made no sense. Even after I was able to speak again and was able to function unaided I would often find myself thinking, "Why? What was the purpose of it all?"

Perhaps you're currently facing difficult circumstances and you're wondering when it's all going to end? You might have gone through difficult times, and weathered many storms in life – in your finances, your marriage, your work, or other relationships. Perhaps your pain and hurt are not something of the past, but are a tangible reality in your life right now. I urge you with all my heart not to give up and despair. Think about Joshua who stood at the edge of the Jordan River, or Joseph who was imprisoned as a slave. Nothing made sense to them either. Job's words, found in Job 23 in The Message, have taken on a whole new meaning for me:

> *If I knew where on earth to find him, I'd go straight to him. I'd lay my case before him face-to-face, give him all my arguments first-hand. I'd find out exactly what he's thinking, discover what's going on in his head. Do you think he'd dismiss me or bully me? No, he'd take me seriously. He'd see a straight-living man standing before him; my Judge would acquit me for good of all charges. I travel East looking for him - I find no one; then West, but not a trace; I go North, but he's hidden his tracks; then South, but not even a glimpse.* (Job 23:3-9, The Message)

Job's life-journey did not make sense to him. I believe we tend to be blinded by adversity when it comes our way. Many times during my illness I thought, "Lord, where are You?" I told you about the fever I developed while we were on vacation. I sent my friend a text message in the hope of getting some sympathy from him. His answer, of course, was that I needed to praise and worship God.

Praise and worship was the last thing on my mind at that point but the Bible tells us that is exactly what Job did! When bad news hit him from all sides, the Bible said he got up, tore his clothes, shaved his head, fell on the ground and worshiped God.

How will you respond if the same things that happened to Job happened to you? Like Job, will you choose to worship and praise God despite your circumstances? Will you show patience and longsuffering or will you give up and despair?

This may sound quite hopeless to you, but when I was ill I often felt really lonely and that I had lost all focus. If I think back on those times now, I realize that my focus was entirely on my pain and discomfort. I focused on myself to the extent that I forgot to praise and worship God for who He is. When I share this with people, many have told me that I'm only human and it's human to focus on your pain and discomfort so I shouldn't be so hard on myself.

While this may be true, we were made to worship God. The real question should be: what is the focus of our worship? Will we worship our own man-made universe where we are in control, or will we worship the Almighty God of the universe who is all-powerful and in control of everything? We need to worship Him even if we don't understand the circumstances we find ourselves in. A few years ago a much-loved member of our congregation died shortly after an operation. I couldn't understand why this had happened. Many people asked, "WHY?" and others even insisted that God owed us an explanation. Does God really owe us an answer? Or is this essentially what makes Him God?

Read with me from Isaiah 25:1, Hebrews 1:3 and Colossians 1:17-18 in The Message. Here we see that God is our God, that His plans for us are only good; and that He can bring about all things simply by speaking.

GOD, you are my God. I celebrate you. I praise you. You've done your share of miracle-wonders, well-thought-out plans, solid and sure. (Isaiah 25:1, The Message)

This Son [Jesus] perfectly mirrors God, and is stamped with God's nature. He holds everything together by what he says—powerful words! (Hebrews 1:3, The Message)

He was there before any of it came into existence and holds it all together right up to this moment. (Colossians 1:17, The Message)

These verses clearly show us that God is in control of everything. How can I not focus on Him? What did longsuffering mean to me during my illness? It was the joy of not knowing when my healing would be complete. Yes, this may sound strange, but it was a joy to realize that I did not have to be concerned about tomorrow, because I knew that God was in control of my life. This is confirmed in Psalm 115:3:

But our God is in heaven; He does whatever He pleases. (Psalm 115:3, NKJV)

B.B Warfield describes the foundation of our discomfort as follows: *"We wish 'to belong to ourselves,' and we resent belonging, especially belonging absolutely, to anybody else, even if that anybody else be God."* If we would simply surrender ourselves to God and allow Him to become EVERYTHING to us, even discomfort would become a joy instead of a burden.

Stand firm in the Name of the Lord

Read Ephesians 6:10-20 for yourself. This passage teaches us that we need to put on the full armor of God as well as the fact that we do not do battle against flesh and blood, but against the evil principalities and powers of the air. I'd like to start with verse 10:

> *Finally, my brethren,* **be strong in the Lord and in the power of His might.** (Ephesians 6:10, NKJV)

We need to become POWERFUL in the Lord – in other words, the words we speak need to be in line with His Word and our actions should look like His actions. The power we have does not come from ourselves, but from God. You may be weak and inept, but fortunately He is strong. Let's look at the words the Lord gave Joshua when He instructed him to stand firm:

> **Be strong and of good courage,** *for to this people you shall divide as an inheritance the land which I swore to their fathers to give them. Only* **be strong and very courageous,** *that you may observe to do according to all the law which Moses My servant commanded you; do not turn from it to the right hand or to the left, that you may prosper wherever you go. This Book of the Law* **(God's Word, the Living Word)** *shall not depart from your mouth, but you shall meditate in it day and night (think of it often, so that your mind can be renewed), that you may observe to do according to all that is written in it (so that you will understand God's will for your life and arrange your life accordingly). For then you will make your way prosperous, and then you will have good success. Have I not*

commanded you? **Be strong and of good courage; do not be afraid, *nor be dismayed, for the LORD your God is with you wherever you go.*"** (Joshua 1:6-9, NKJV; parentheses mine)

As you read this, declare with me: "Lord, my choice and decision is to follow You, and only You. I will not FEAR any longer. I am STRONG and COURAGEOUS in the name of Jesus."

> **"Lord, my choice and decision is to follow You, and only You. I will not FEAR any longer. I am STRONG and COURA-GEOUS in the name of Jesus."**

Let's go back to Ephesians 6 and read from verse 11:

Put on the whole armor of God, that you may be able to stand against the wiles of the devil. (Ephesians 6:11, NKJV)

The Word is very clear – STAND FIRM in the name of the Lord. He is your rock and your refuge, and He, the Almighty, will shelter you.

For we do not wrestle against flesh and blood, but against principalities, against powers, against the rulers of the darkness of this age, against spiritual hosts of wickedness in the heavenly places. (Ephesians 6:12, NKJV)

The government is not the source of your problems but rather the principalities and powers, the forces of evil and the powers of darkness.

Therefore take up the whole armor of God, that you may be able to withstand in the evil day, and having done all, to stand. Stand therefore, having girded your waist with truth, having put on the breastplate of righteousness, and having shod your feet with the preparation of the gospel of peace. (Ephesians 6:13-15, NKJV)

PEACE opens doors. PEACE brings GOOD news to BAD places. It is the GOODNESS OF GOD that leads people to JESUS, not judgment, bullying or protests. It is the GOODNESS OF GOD that changes people's lives.

PEACE opens doors. PEACE brings GOOD news to BAD places.

Above all, taking the shield of faith with which you will be able to quench all the fiery darts of the wicked one. (Ephesians 6:16, NKJV)

Trusting in the GOODNESS OF GOD causes His joy to surround you and you will be able to hold up your shield of faith against the powers of the enemy.

And take the helmet of salvation, and the sword of the Spirit, which is the word of God. (Ephesians 6:17, NKJV)

You need to renew your mind – a whole new way of thinking. You need to receive His Sozo (spiritual well-being). Receive the

GOSPEL (good news) of which you don't have to be ashamed.

... praying always with all prayer and supplication in the Spirit, being watchful to this end with all perseverance and supplication for all the saints. (Ephesians 6:18, NKJV)

To live like this means TRULY LIVING IN THE SPIRIT. The Greek word for this is *Zoe*. Andrew Wommack describes this with reference to John 10:10:

The Greek word translated "life" here is ZOE, and it means "life in the absolute sense, life as God has it" (Vine's Expository Dictionary). Everyone who is breathing has life in the sense of physical existence, but only those who receive Jesus can experience life as God intended it to be. Jesus came not only to save people from the torment of eternal hell but also to give them this ZOE life, or God-kind of life, in abundance. The life of God is not awaiting people in heaven but is the present possession of all born-again believers in their spirits (John 5:24 and 1 John 3:14). Believers can release this ZOE life and enjoy it now by losing their natural lives (Matthew 16:24-25, Mark 8:34-37, and Luke 9:23-25) and finding this supernatural life. The way believers lose their lives is to deny any thoughts, emotions, or actions that are contrary to the Word of God, which is life (ZOE in John 6:63). When they line their thoughts, emotions, and actions up with the instructions of God's Word, then they'll find this ZOE life manifest in their bodies and souls as well.

... and for me, that utterance may be given to me, that I may open my mouth boldly to make known the mystery of the gospel, for which I am an ambassador in chains; that in it I may speak boldly, **as I ought to speak.** (Ephesians 6:19 - 20, NKJV)

This is why you and I need to SPEAK and DECLARE THE WORD over our circumstances.

Once I was really desperate to find a solution to an issue I was dealing with. I picked up the Word and began to read. I truly believe that the Word is like water. It cleanses your system and your thoughts from the world's dirt and its lack of faith. I began to read from Mark 4 and when I got to chapter 7, these words suddenly stood out for me:

This people honors Me with their lips, but their heart is far from Me. (Mark 7:6, NKJV)

The Lord is saying that man-made religions are illusions, because people hold up these man-made dogmas as Divine Laws. We can never settle for simple sounding religion and make all the right spiritual noises by saying things like, "You know, God's plan is not our plan. He has a plan with everything..." When we speak in this way, we are agreeing with the SPIRIT of this world. We could then be described as having a form of godliness, but we deny its power (see 2 Timothy 3:1-5).

As I continued reading the Gospel of Mark, I discovered that it's not what I eat or drink that defiles my life, but rather what I allow or tolerate in my thoughts. Negative words affect my thinking. They are like weeds that compete with the good seed. Jesus said:

There is nothing that enters a man from outside which can defile him; but the things which come out of him, those are the things that defile a man. (Mark 7:15, NKJV)

Jesus emphatically states that what you eat or drink won't defile you, but what you talk about will. We also read in the book of Mark that the mouth speaks from the overflow of the heart. The question we need to ask is, "What does your 'language' sound like?" Do you frequently hear the following in the way you speak?

- Do you often complain?
- Are you ungrateful?
- Are you never satisfied with what you have?
- Do you compare yourself with others?
- Do you speak negative words?

This is simply the fruit of a heart filled with the world's negative words, leaving no room to see and experience the supernatural realm of God.

In Mark 8 we read the awesome account of how Jesus miraculously multiplied the seven loaves of bread and a few fish in order to feed four thousand people. The most amazing of all was that after everyone had eaten enough, seven baskets of food were gathered as leftovers. After this happened, Jesus and His disciples got into a boat and went to the other side of the lake where they met a group of Pharisees. These Pharisees had not experienced the miracle that Jesus had just performed, and they were just out to cause trouble. In Mark 8 we read:

Then the Pharisees came out and began to dispute with Him, seeking from Him a sign from heaven, testing Him. (Mark 8:11, NKJV)

In the King James Version we read that they questioned and tempted Him, and the Living Bible uses the word "argue". Clearly the Pharisees were not looking to have a friendly conversation with Jesus. They also insisted that Jesus perform a miracle for them as a sign. The disciples were excited as they'd just experienced Jesus performing the incredible multiplication miracle. Perhaps they said something like, "Yes, Lord, show them! Do something that will take their breath away." But Jesus responded differently:

> *But He sighed deeply in His spirit, and said, "Why does this generation seek a sign? Assuredly, I say to you, no sign shall be given to this generation."* (Mark 8:12, NKJV)

Jesus did not want to perform a miracle, because He knew that it did not matter what these people saw or heard – they still would not believe. Religion, as the Pharisees practiced it, makes you blind and deaf. Only a living relationship with Jesus releases God's life within you.

Jesus and His disciples then went back to the boat, but the disciples were unhappy. They wanted Jesus to prove a point, to show His power. You could say they had the spirit of Herod and of the Pharisees on them. The example I am about to use is not to judge people who smoke but simply to illustrate my point. Across the world smoking nicotine is regarded as unhealthy. We also know that secondary smoke is as dangerous, or perhaps even more dangerous than smoking itself. My point is - you don't have to smoke to smell of smoke; you only need to stand close to someone who smokes. The same thing happens when people are dissatisfied – you don't have to fight and make a noise to be part of the argument – you only need to be around it for it to affect you. Do you still remember what Romans 10:8 says? *"The word is near you, in your mouth and in your heart"* (that is, the word of faith which we preach) ... Back to my story – His disciples allowed the spirit of strife from the Pharisees to rub off on them, and they totally forgot to buy bread. Perhaps it was stingy, stealing Judas who made them forget to buy bread? Let's read from Mark 8:14-21.

Now the disciples had forgotten to take bread, and they did not have more than one loaf with them in the boat. Then He charged them, saying, "Take heed, beware of the leaven of the Pharisees and the leaven of Herod." (Mark 8:14-15, NKJV)

When Jesus spoke to his disciples, he warned them to be careful of the leaven (the yeast) of the Pharisees. Yeast is a unicellular fungus that breaks down carbohydrates into carbon dioxide and alcohol during the process of fermentation. There are different types of yeast – baker's yeast probably being the most well-known. Only a tiny bit of yeast is needed to infiltrate a large quantity of dough and give it a very distinct taste. A small quantity of yeast actually takes over the whole piece of dough. Jesus warned his disciples not to tolerate the Pharisees' way of thinking, because just like yeast, those thoughts could infiltrate their thinking and take over their minds. The Pharisees represent the religious system. They believed in the existence of God and that we should honor Him, but they also believed that God has no power. God is the ceremonial head of Heaven and Earth, but cannot really achieve anything in the spirit. Today we see the same Pharisaical tendency among some people who call themselves believers. They believe in a powerless God who still enforces a system of morality on earth. Herod's yeast, on the other hand, is an atheistic influence based on the power of man-made constructs like systems, politics, popular opinion and beliefs. A writer once said that the yeast of Herod permeates the worldly culture. He went on to say that the Western world in particular is made up of self-made people, pioneers who believe that they can achieve anything they set their minds to purely by their own resolve, discipline and administrative excellence.

> *And they reasoned among themselves, saying, "It is because we have no bread."* (Mark 8:16, NKJV)

I have mentioned previously that we need to live in unity with one another, always guarding the peace because when we move out of harmony, the enemy sees the opportunity to come in and destroy our lives and relationships. That's exactly what he was doing among the disciples at this point in the story – he caused them to argue with each other.

> *But Jesus, being aware of it, said to them, "Why do you reason because you have no bread? Do you not yet perceive nor understand? Is your heart still hardened?* **Having eyes, do you not see? And having ears, do you not hear?** *And do you not remember?* (Mark 8:17-18, NKJV)

Jesus confronted his disciples, and asked them, "Can't you SEE or HEAR? Have you so easily forgotten what I have just done? Have you forgotten Who is in this boat with you?"

> *When I broke the five loaves for the five thousand, how many baskets full of fragments did you take up?" They said to Him, "Twelve."* (Mark 8:19, NKJV)

5 Loaves = 12 Baskets full

"Also, when I broke the seven for the four thousand, how many large baskets full of fragments did you take up?" And they said, "Seven." (Mark 8:20, NKJV)

7 Loaves = 7 Baskets full

So He said to them, "How is it you do not understand?" (Mark 8:19, NKJV)

I think Jesus said to them, "Listen up, I'm the Lord of multiplication. Where did you learn to do math? Didn't anyone tell you of the X-factor?" 1 Loaf is usually enough for 13 people and yet Jesus fed thousands with a few loaves. He wanted to teach them to recognize that food multiplies when He is at the center. If they understood this principle, they would be able to multiply food wherever they went. I want to share this testimony from Heidi Baker with you – it's about food that miraculously multiplied:

In 1995 Heidi arrived with her family in Mozambique – the poorest country in the world. The government offered them a horribly dilapidated "orphanage". After a brutal civil war had been raging there for many years, thousands of children were orphaned, displaced and simply left to get by on their own.

There were 80 kids in the orphanage, and God released His love over them, providing food every day. A church was planted and hundreds of people turned to God. The erstwhile communist directors of the government orphanage were livid when Heidi and her husband took over the orphanage, because then these directors' terrible corruption and stealing had to come to an end. The directors sided with another corrupt faction of the government and made up accusations against Heidi and her family. Then they got a court order against Iris Ministries in which they prohibited all prayer and worship, Christian singing and all sources of "unapproved" food and clothing distribution, and all medical assistance.

Since Heidi and her family did not heed the order, they were given 48 hours to leave the property. Heidi was also informed that a contract was out on her life – she was in great personal danger. Heidi and her family left for their head office in Maputo. The kids gathered in the dining room/church section and sang songs of worship as loud as they could. They were beaten and told that they were not allowed to praise God. One by one they set out on the 20-mile journey to the city. Once they'd been united with Heidi and Rolland, Heidi, Rolland and the orphans desperately called out to God.

They'd lost everything; they had no place to stay and there was nothing to eat. A friend of the US Embassy came over with a pot of rice and some chili sauce for the Bakers and their two kids. They prayed over the food and told the 80+ kids to sit down. Each of them received food and ate until they've had enough! God graced their faith with supernatural favor. Today, their property i-Pemba is seven times the size it used to be when they lost it in 1997.

Heidi once said, "Government officials who once persecuted us and who beat our kids are now thankful that we are in the country."

Jesus also wants to teach you the same principles through hearing these testimonies and reading the scriptures. He is able to take whatever you have in your hand and kill a giant with it. Whatever you have in your hand right now, God does the following:

- He feeds thousands of people.
- He provides for the needs of you and your family, and your town according to your faith.
- He receives your thankfulness and heals people from incurable diseases.
- He takes your actions and grows a town's economy through them.
- If there's no school for you to teach at, He will have a school built for you.
- If the kinds of people you need in your congregation aren't in town, He will bring them from faraway places.
- He makes gold where there was nothing.
- He brings rain over the desert and turns it into a beautiful garden.
- He makes your current salary your tithe.
- He heals your children even though the doctor said, "Sorry, it is impossible".

WITH MY GOD I SCALE OVER A WALL.
With My GOD the IMOSSIBLE becomes POSSIBLE.

Praise the LORD because HE IS GOOD AND HIS GOODNESS ENDURES FOREVER.

We are almost at the end of our journey of faith. In this book it has become clear that we serve an UNLIMITED GOD. We serve a God who wants to bless us in abundance. We serve a God who makes THE IMPOSSIBLE POSSIBLE. I'd like to end with Hebrews 12:1-3 in two different versions.

Therefore we also, since we are surrounded by so great a cloud of witnesses, let us lay aside every weight, and the sin which so easily ensnares us, and let us run with endurance the race that is set before us, looking unto Jesus, the author and finisher of our faith, who for the joy that was set before Him endured the cross, despising the shame, and has sat down at the right hand of the throne of God. For consider Him who endured such hostility from sinners against Himself, lest you become weary and discouraged in your souls. (Hebrews 12:1-3, NKJV)

WITH MY GOD I SCALE OVER A WALL With My GOD the IMOSSIBLE becomes POSSIBLE.

And

"So now the stage is set for us: all these faith-heroes cheer us on, as it were, like a great multitude of spectators in the amphitheater. This is our moment. As with an athlete who is determined to win, it would be silly to carry any baggage of the old law-system that would weigh one down. Make sure you do not get your feet clogged up with sin-consciousness. Become absolutely streamlined in faith. Run the race of your spiritual life with total persuasion. (Persuaded in the success of the cross). Look away from the shadow dispensation of the law and the prophets and fix your eyes upon Jesus. He is the fountainhead and conclusion of faith. He saw the joy (of mankind's salvation) when he braved the cross and despised the shame

of it. As the executive authority of God (the right hand of the Throne of God) he now occupies the highest seat of dominion to endorse man's innocence! (Having accomplished purification of sins, he sat down. [Heb. 1:3, Isa. 53:11]). Ponder how he overcame all the odds stacked against him, this will boost your soul-energy when you feel exhausted. (The Mirror Bible)

Many people think when they get to know Jesus and get saved, that they've come to the end of their spiritual journey. Nothing could be further from the truth, because getting to know Jesus is only the beginning. It's the beginning of your life-long journey of faith. Fortunately it is not a lonely journey - there are many heroes of faith who are watching us and encouraging us. In the Living Bible, we read about a "huge crowd of men of faith watching us from the grandstands." Imagine a huge sports stadium filled with people. Not just any people mind you – quality people. People whose names are inscribed on God's memorial wall – Abel, Enoch, Noah, Abraham, Isaac, Jacob, Sarah and many others. They are all there to encourage you to keep going until you reach the finish line. How do you stay focused on the finish line?

- Know that there are people who've completed the journey of life and faith successfully. Our most important example is Jesus who is called the Finisher of our faith journey.
- Prepare to run your race effectively and know that you're embarking on a life-long journey. Get rid of whatever may derail or distract you along the way, or whatever might detain you unnecessarily. An athlete doesn't put on all the clothes in his wardrobe and then attempt to win a race. NO! He dresses himself in appropriate clothing that will make him run the race effectively. Don't get caught up in the sins of the world.

Run with perseverance and persistence, and don't allow the realities of the world to discourage you.

- Focus on Jesus and not on yourself or the many people around you. Remember when Peter walked on water? When he kept his eyes on Jesus, everything went well, but the moment he shifted his focus onto his circumstances (the waves around him), he began to sink!

- Be strong and courageous, don't give up – complete the journey! The world is often against you when you follow Jesus, but that's really only a temporary obstacle. The Lord told Joshua many times to be strong and courageous, to be brave. Jesus is also telling you today to be strong, courageous and brave. Don't give up!

In your mind, go back to the image of the sports stadium. Picture the heroes of faith, all gathered together, shouting their support and cheering you on. Someone is waiting for you at the finish line – JESUS and His encouragement is stronger, more powerful and more meaningful than all the heroes of faith together. Remember – the journey of faith is not over until you stand before Jesus!

> *Even the youths shall faint and be weary, and the young men shall utterly fall,* **but those who wait on the LORD Shall renew their strength;** *they shall mount up with wings like eagles, they shall run and not be weary, they shall walk and not faint.*
> (Isaiah 40:30-31, NKJV)

I have reached the end of my faith journey with you. This book has covered many aspects of faith, but I would like to leave you with these final thoughts: We have all received a measure of faith. In the same way a sportsman or woman needs to exercise in order to develop strong, well-built muscles, we need to exercise

God says, "Believe and you will see" and it is when we believe that God TURNS THE IMPOSSIBLE INTO THE POSSIBLE!

our faith muscles. This means that faith is not passive, but active – it needs to be exercised and developed! Faith makes you think differently; makes you speak differently and see things differently to the world. A worldly perspective often makes us believe there is no future, but faith enables you to experience the future in the now. The world says, "Seeing is believing." However, God says, "Believe and you will see" and it is when we believe that God TURNS THE IMPOSSIBLE INTO THE POSSIBLE!

Now faith is the substance of things hoped for, the evidence of things not seen. (Hebrews 11:1, NKJV)

Literature Used

1
Hagin, K.E. 2006. Bible Faith – Study Course. Rhema Bible Church, USA

Warren, R. 10/11/2000. 50 Days of Faith – Mid Week are the five midweek lessons delivered during the 50 Days of Faith series first taught at Saddleback in the Fall of 2000. I would highly recommend this as a very good resource: http://www.saddlebackresources.com/50-Days-of-Faith-5Transcripts-P8265.aspx

2
Pieterse, A. 2013. Die Groter Prentjie. Printing Things, Potchefstroom.

4
Wommack, A. 1997. The Faith of God. http://www.awmi.net/extra/article/faith_god

5
Anonymous. 2013. Crime Stats Simplified. http://www.crimestatssa.com/didyouknow.php

Dollar, C. 1993. "The Divine Order of Faith" 1993 World Changers Ministries, College Park, Georgia, USA

6
Copeland, K. 2006. Now that we are in Christ Jesus. ©2006 Kenneth Copeland Ministries, Incorporated, Kenneth Copeland Publications Fort Worth, Texas

Cordeiro, W. 2001. The Divine Mentor by Bethany House Publishers

Du Toit, Francois. 2006. God believes in you. Mirrorreflection.net.

Kenyon, E.W. & Gossett, D. 2009. Words that move Mountains. Whitaker House.

7
Capps, C. 2009. The Tongue, a creative force. Capps publishing.

8

Copeland, K. 2009-2014. Faith Series. Learn to release God's power through faith, develop and apply faith, and use the Word to rule over your circumstances (CD Series).
Gosset, D. & Kenyon, E.W. 2009. Words that move mountains. Whitaker House, New Kensington, PA
Stanley, A. Breathing room series Podcast: 2013, North Point Ministries, Inc, www.northpointministries.org, 4350, North Point Parkway, Alpharetta, GA, 30022

9

Baker, H. 2014. Intimacy for Miracles. http://www.cbn.com/700club/guests/bios/heidi_baker081208.aspx
Wommack, A. 2014. John 10:10. http://www.awmi.net/bible/joh_10_10

The following book was used as literature source in various chapters in this book::
Nel, W.2009. A Silent Adventure. Faith Story Publishing, Potchefstroom

ABOUT THE ATHOUR

WILLEM IS THE LEAD PASTOR OF His People Faith City – a multi-cultural, multi-generational and multi-site church based in Potchefstroom, Klerksdorp and Parys, South Africa. He also serves on the Apostolic Board of Every Nation South Africa. (His People belong to a wider family of churches called Every Nation). He is the founder of Faith Story Publishing, a publishing house dedicated to making God famous by telling faith stories of ordinary believers who have a passion to share the good news all over the world. Willem has published two books. A Silent Adventure, telling his remarkable story of healing and adventure into grace, was his first inspirational book published by Faith Story Publishing.

Willem is a motivational speaker, preacher and executive life coach. His life is marked with a strong word of faith, with healings and miracles a part of his ministry. He lives in Potchefstroom, South Africa and along with other leaders is involved with the transformation of the region.

Willem graduated from RAU with a BCOMM (Accountancy) in 1988. He was awarded his BCOMM Hons from UNISA in 1996 and his Masters in Organizational Leadership (Cum Laude) from Regent University in the USA. He has written three publications on leadership which includes: Moving a Church from Good to Great; SHAPE for Business Leaders and Church Health Matrix.

Willem ministers regularly locally, nationally and abroad. He has strong ties with various congregations in the USA who invite him to minister. In the last few years he has ministered in several churches and at various conferences.

Back: Charmoré, Willem, Celesté en Guilliam
Front: Ann-waniq en D'Ianrew

Willem is happily married to Celesté and they have four beautiful children, Guilliam, Charmoré, Ann-waniq and D'Ianrew. As a family, their mission is to see lives impacted by the Good news of Jesus Christ. Together they have ministered all over South Africa, in Botswana, The Philippines and the USA. Celesté is one of the Teaching Pastors at His People Faith City. Guilliam is currently studying Ministry leadership at Oral Roberts University, Tulsa Oklahoma. Charmoré is actively involved with the Worship ministry and currently leads a Youth Band.

Contact Details:

Email: nelwillem@gmail.com
Phone: +27 18 297 8229
Website: www.hispeople.co.za

www.facebook.com/nelwillem
www.twitter.com/nelwillem

ABOUT THE SHADOW WRITER

FRANCI JORDAAN IS A WIFE TO DIETER AND MOM to her two daughters, Claudine and Tanya, an academic and a brilliant researcher with a passion for writing. She acts as translator, language editor and shadow writer for Faith Story Publishing. She has already been involved in many projects, transforming loose thoughts into phenomenal stories.

In this book, Making The Impossible Possible, Franci helped me re-write my sermons and blogs into book form that will touch thousands of people's lives. A unique partnership has emerged from writing this book together. I would never have been able to do it on my own.

I am convinced there are thousands of people, who, like me have a lot of thoughts but don't know how to turn them into a book. I recommend Franci for any project. You can contact her at franci@faithstory.co.za

Made in the USA
Columbia, SC
10 July 2023

20038256R00167